GREEN INVESTMENT BANKS
UNLEASHING THE POTENTIAL OF NATIONAL DEVELOPMENT BANKS TO FINANCE A GREEN AND JUST TRANSITION

Ulrich Volz, Junkyu Lee

JUNE 2024

ASIAN DEVELOPMENT BANK

Notes:
ADB recognizes "China" as the People's Republic of China; "Hong Kong" as Hong Kong, China; "Korea" as the Republic of Korea; and "Vietnam" as Viet Nam.

In this publication, "$" refers to United States dollars , "£" refers to pounds sterling,"¥" refers to yen, "B" refers to baht, "KR" refers to riels, and "RM" refers to ringgit.

On the cover: Green investment banks. National development banks have the potential to finance a green and just transition through the establishment of green investment banks (photo by ADB).

Contents

Tables, Figures, and Boxes

Foreword

As our world navigates unprecedented environmental challenges, it is time to fully leverage the financial strengths of public financial institutions to further the objectives of the international accords, including the Paris Agreement, designed to mitigate climate change.

A pressing issue is the shortfall in long-term finance for climate projects. These have trouble attracting investment given their perception as risky, overly long-term, and carrying uncertain returns. Private capital, inherently conservative, risk-averse, and focused on short-term returns, cannot fill the gap, now widely estimated at trillions of dollars a year.

Green investment banks offer a promising way forward. More broadly focused public development banks—now numbering more than 500 subnational, national, regional, and global institutions—already contribute 10%–12% of global investment, with around $2.4 trillion in annual lending and $23 trillion in assets. While significant, this amount is not proportionate to our planet's pressing needs as our economies need to transition to net-zero emissions.

The huge investment needed and the challenges mobilizing private capital thus necessitate a larger, greener role for public banks and funds. Their potential for financing a green transition remains largely untapped, and the repositioning of at least some of them as green investment banks, or establishing new ones from scratch, could substantially boost climate finance.

This publication underscores the potential for green investment banks to finance a green and just transition, making a case for strengthening their role and showing how international development finance institutions can help unleash their potential. It is indeed critical that these institutions emerge as powerful and cost-effective vehicles to overcome investment barriers, leverage available resources, and help localize the Sustainable Development Goals.

Given the enormity of the investments needed in emerging markets and developing economies for climate mitigation and adaptation, this publication presents an urgent call for action. It paints a picture of the potential that lies within the framework of green finance, and the role of public financial institutions.

The multilateral development institutions, including the Asian Development Bank, have a major role to play. A 2022 review of capital adequacy frameworks argues that these institutions could unleash hundreds of billions of dollars in new lending if they were to adjust their capital adequacy frameworks and maximize the impact of their capital.

Indeed, some institutions are taking up the call to evolve into "green" or "climate banks". ADB and other multilaterals can use their deep knowledge of developing countries and innovative technical assistance to support developing country governments as they consider the green investment bank option. And this policy brief can be a crucial catalyst in mobilizing action for sustainable finance for a greener, more inclusive, and resilient world.

Acknowledgments

Green Investment Banks: Unleashing the Potential of National Development Banks to Finance a Green and Just Transition is a product of the Finance Sector Office of the Asian Development Bank (ADB). This report was prepared as part of ADB's support to knowledge work on underscoring the potential for green investment banks to finance a green and just transition, making a case for strengthening their role and showing how international development finance institutions can help unleash their potential.

The publication was co-authored by Ulrich Volz, professor of economics and director of the Centre for Sustainable Finance at SOAS, University of London, and Junkyu Lee, director of the Finance Sector Office, ADB.

Both provided the expertise and knowledge for jointly developing this study. Volz instilled high-level inputs and leading international experience into the study. Lee provided comprehensive input as the second author and headed a core team of staff in preparing the publication.

Special thanks go to Bruno Carrasco, director general of the Climate Change and Sustainable Development Department for his strong support and detailed guidance in setting the direction of the paper and enhancing the quality of the study.

The draft was enriched by the former Finance Sector Committee members of the Finance Sector Group in ADB (Christine Engstrom, Tariq Niazi, Xiaoqin Fan, Jose Antonio Tan, Sabyasachi Mitra, Lotte Schou-Zibell, Satoru Yamadera, Jonathan Grosvenor). Sung Su Kim, senior financial sector specialist, has led the coordination on the production of the publication and never spared his effort to play a key role to ensure the production with the author and the group of contributors. Katherine Mitzi Co, associate operations analyst, and Matilde Mila Cauinian provided gracious administrative support.

For endorsement, support, and guidance in this knowledge product, the team wishes to acknowledge Ramesh Subramaniam, director general and group chief; Sungsup Ra, deputy director general and deputy group chief of Sector Group; and the members of the former Finance Sector Group Committee of ADB.

The drafting team is also grateful for the support of Christine Engstrom, senior director of the Finance Sector Office. She provided invaluable comments in the May 2023 international conference and encouraged the team to pitch in effort to reflect perspectives of developing member countries and private sector financial institutions.

We thank all contributors for their valiant support of this publication and acknowledge colleagues from the Department of Communications and Knowledge Management for their continuous support in disseminating the publication.

Finally, this publication benefited substantially from the contributions of policy makers from ADB developing member countries, representatives from green investment banks and ADB staff who attended the conference, gave presentations, and engaged in active discussions to develop and refine the publication:

Chowdhury Liakat Ali, director for Sustainable Finance Department, Bangladesh Bank

Adi Budiarso, director for Center for Financial Sector, Ministry of Finance, Indonesia

Bert Hunter, executive vice president and chief investment officer, Connecticut Green Bank

Adrian Barnes, head of Green Analytics, Green Investment Group, Macquarie Asset Management

Pavit Ramachandran, country director of ADB Mongolia Resident Mission

Anjum Israr, senior public management specialist at Central and West Asia Department, ADB

Abbreviations

ADB	Asian Development Bank
AFD	Agence Française de Développement
ASEAN	Association of Southeast Asian Nations
CEFIA	Clean Energy Finance and Investment Authority
CGB	Connecticut Green Bank
C-PACE	Commercial Property Assessed Clean Energy
GCF	Green Climate Fund
GIBs	green investment banks
GTFS	Green Technology Financing Scheme
MDBs	multilateral development banks
MSMEs	micro, small, and medium-sized enterprises
OECD	Organisation for Economic Co-operation and Development
PCG	partial credit guarantee
PDBs	public development banks
SDGs	Sustainable Development Goals
UNDP	United Nations Development Programme
UNESCAP	United Nations Economic and Social Commission for Asia and the Pacific
UK GIB	United Kingdom Green Investment Bank

Executive Summary

The need is urgent for more sustainable finance and investment to achieve the Paris Agreement climate targets and the 2030 Agenda for Sustainable Development. Commercial financial institutions are limited in providing long-term finance, especially for activities with uncertain returns and positive externalities. As such, recognition is growing that public financial institutions need to play a greater role in scaling up investment in climate action and the Sustainable Development Goals (SDGs).

Public development banks already play a critical role at the multilateral, regional, national, and subnational levels. With the great magnitude of investment required to finance the transition to low-carbon, net-zero economies and the challenges in mobilizing private capital, public banks, and funds ought to play a large role, both in developing and advanced economies.

Calls are intensifying for a greater role for multilateral development banks (MDBs) and national development banks as these institutions can support structural transformation and the implementation of sustainable economic models. While national development banks often play an important role in their domestic economies already, their potential to finance and accelerate a green and just transition has been mostly untapped. It is important to consider how to turn such institutions into green investment banks (GIBs). A GIB is a publicly capitalized entity that facilitates private investment into domestic infrastructure and other green sectors.

Emerging markets and developing economies need enormous investment for climate mitigation and adaptation; for better and more inclusive economic, social, and ecological conditions; and to achieve the SDGs. The successful implementation of low-emission development strategies and national adaptation plans or national adaptation programs of action can only be achieved if domestic resource mobilization is strengthened. Thus, leveraging private finance for climate and sustainable development through public banks ought to be part of the solution using tried-and-tested methods of leveraging private sector finance for development.

With the investment barriers and the market failure that public development banks need to overcome to finance structural transformation to sustainable development, GIBs use targeted approaches and tailored financial structuring to address the lack of suitable low-carbon climate-resilient investments with attributes sought by private investors. They also address a shortage of objective information, data, and skills to assess transactions and underlying risks. Moreover, GIBs can work with governments to create favorable framework conditions for green investments and help develop a project pipeline of green investable projects.

The actual number of GIBs and GIB-like entities in operation is still small; thus, the rationale is strong for either transforming existing public development banks into GIBs or creating entirely new institutions. The former can be achieved by updating the mandates of public development banks to focus on a just, net-zero transition and possibly link this with a capital increase. New GIBs can be capitalized through governments, central banks, MDBs/development finance institutions, and global funds, and require both political/financial capital and time. Dedicated GIBs require commitment from leadership and staff to the mission of financing green transition armed with expertise in sustainable finance and green economy.

International development finance institutions can support the establishment of new GIBs and help existing national development banks reinvent themselves as GIBs. They can do this by offering technical assistance to build strong governance structures and providing capital or credit enhancements to enable GIBs to obtain higher ratings to refinance themselves at more favorable conditions or by passing on concessionary financing to GIBs. Also, MDB lending through financial intermediation loans can provide nascent green investment banks access to low-cost finance.

The cases of the Connecticut Green Bank, the UK Green Investment Bank, and GIB-like entities such as Malaysia's Green Technology Financing Scheme (GTFS) and Japan's Green Fund and Green Innovation Fund are discussed in this paper. Being the first green bank in the United States, the Connecticut Green Bank upended the government subsidy-driven approach to clean energy by working with private-sector investors to create low-cost, long-term sustainable financing to maximize the use of public funds. It also continues to innovate, educate, and activate to accelerate the growth of green energy measures, leading to a deployment of over $2.2 billion in capital for clean energy projects across the state with the help of its private investment partners.

The UK Green Investment Bank, in its five-year operation before being privatized in 2017, financed more than £12 billion of green infrastructure projects to comply with an explicit mandate of accelerating the United Kingdom's (UK) transition to a greener, stronger economy by investing in green projects and mobilizing private finance into the green energy sector. UK GIB was set up as an enduring institution with sound corporate governance that operates at arm's length from the government.

Malaysia's GTFS is operated by the Malaysian Green Technology and Climate Change Centre which provides loan guarantees and subsidies to encourage private banks to finance green projects. They also assess eligible companies' applications for green project certificates that they also issue. While not a full-fledged GIB, GTFS's lending has been accompanied by other public incentives and policies and has enhanced green lending and investment in Malaysia by working with commercial banks.

Japan's Green Fund commenced operations following the announcement to build a low-carbon society that highlights the need to use private capital to tackle global warming. It was specifically established to address the challenges associated with clean energy projects, as well as to solidify the business case of small- to large-scale clean energy projects by making equity and mezzanine investments that attract further capital from private sources to reduce greenhouse gases and create a decarbonized society. On the other hand, Japan's Green Innovation Fund was launched following the carbon neutrality goal in the Japanese economy by 2050. It funds research and development and social implementation activities that can deliver technological advances that will help the net-zero transition with shared goals between the public and private sectors.

Public development banks and GIBs will have to play a key role in closing the gap in investment and SDG financing gap in Asia and the Pacific. Careful analysis is required, whether attempts at transforming an existing institution into a GIB are likely to succeed, as not all national development banks are operating successfully, and not all can be transformed into successful GIBs. International development finance institutions should consider establishing support programs for either of these endeavors. Also, MDBs and national development banks must create an enabling environment and a reliable framework to catalyze green investments and streamline their projects that target green finance while overcoming market failures.

Towards this end, GIBs can transform the financial sector by becoming powerful and cost-effective vehicles that can support overcoming investment barriers and leveraging the impact of available public and private resources to scale up green investments in Asia and the Pacific.

I. Introduction

The need is urgent for more sustainable finance and investment to achieve the Paris Agreement climate targets and the 2030 Agenda for Sustainable Development. Commercial financial institutions are limited in providing long-term finance, especially for activities with uncertain returns and positive externalities. As such, recognition is growing that public financial institutions need to play a greater role in scaling up investment in climate action and the Sustainable Development Goals (SDGs).

Public development banks already play a critical role at the multilateral, regional, national, and subnational levels. With more than $23 trillion in assets and around $2.4 trillion of annual lending, they finance about 10%–12% of global investment (AFD 2022, Marodon 2022, Griffith-Jones 2022). The great magnitude of investment required to finance the transition to low-carbon, net-zero economies—to limit the rise in average global temperature to 1.5C° above pre-industrial levels—and the challenges in mobilizing private capital suggest an even larger role for public banks and funds in developing and advanced economies.

Globally and regionally, calls have intensified for a greater role for multilateral development banks (MDBs).[1] As recently highlighted in the Independent Review of Multilateral Development Banks' Capital Adequacy Frameworks (Boosting MDBs' Investing Capacity 2022), these institutions could unleash hundreds of billions of dollars in new lending if they were to adjust their capital adequacy frameworks and maximize the impact of their capital. Moreover, member governments can strengthen the firepower of MDBs with general capital increases and a rechanneling of Special Drawing Rights from advanced economies that do not need them. Stronger MDBs should be accompanied by meaningful governance reforms so they can fulfill their potential (e.g., Chakrabarti et al. 2022). Importantly, the MDBs need updated mandates to turn them into "green banks" or "climate banks." In 2018, the Asian Development Bank (ADB) committed to supporting climate action in at least 75% of its operations, with a cumulative climate finance target of at least $80 billion by 2030 (raised to $100 billion in 2021). ADB is also projecting itself now as "Asia and the Pacific's Climate Bank." In November 2019, the European Investment Bank's Board of Directors decided to transform the bank—the world's biggest renewable lender—from a "bank supporting climate" into a "climate bank" and adopted the Climate Bank Roadmap the year after (EIB 2020). Other MDBs need to follow these examples and step up their efforts to become drivers of change.

---

[1] There are also proposals to establish new global funds and facilities for climate and the SDGs to complement MDB financing. Kraemer, Volz, and Schoenmaker (2022) propose a new finance facility against climate change.

National development banks are also receiving increasing attention as institutions that can support structural transformation and the implementation of sustainable economic models (e.g., Sims et al. 2017, Marois 2021, Marodon 2022, Griffith-Jones 2022, Finance in Common and UNDP 2022). While national development banks often play an important role in their domestic economies already, their potential to finance and accelerate a green and just transition has been mostly untapped. It is hence important to consider how to turn such existing institutions into green investment banks (GIBs) or how such banks can be established nationally or subnationally.

As public or nonprofit financial institutions with a dedicated mandate to finance a green and just transition, GIBs can assume a key role in helping finance Agenda 2030. The Organisation for Economic Co-operation and Development (OECD 2016, 15) defines a GIB as "a publicly capitalised entity established specifically to facilitate private investment into domestic [low-carbon, climate-resilient] infrastructure and other green sectors such as water and waste management."[2] Indeed, the interest and momentum to establish GIBs has been growing in recent years. In the United States, the Inflation Reduction Act of December 2023 created national-scale program: the Greenhouse Gas Reduction Fund-a $27 billion investment to mobilize financing and private capital to address the climate crisis. In November 2022, the Green Climate Fund approved a project preparation facility grant to establish the Blue-Green Investment Corporation, a green bank for Barbados, the first in the Caribbean (GCF 2022).

This publication highlights the potential of GIBs to finance a green and just transition. It makes the case for strengthening the role of GIBs and shows how international development finance institutions can help unleash the potential of GIBs in countries of the Global South by helping the establishment of new GIBs or supporting governments in converting existing institutions into GIBs. GIBs can be powerful and cost-effective vehicles to overcome investment barriers and leverage the impact of available public and private resources. More importantly, they can catalyze private operations and capital, scale up climate financing, and localize the SDGs and green operations.

The publication is structured as follows. Section 2 discusses the need to scale up green investment, the financing gap, and the limits to project-based mobilization of private capital. Section 3 makes the case for GIBs. Section 4 discusses key considerations in the development of GIBs. Section 5 discusses how international development finance institutions can support GIBs in the Global South. Section 6 reviews several case studies, Section 7 discusses possible next steps to establish GIBs in developing Asia, and Section 8 concludes.

---

[2]   Schub (2019) defines green banks as "public or nonprofit financial institutions purpose-built to develop, facilitate, and scale investment in greenhouse-gas reducing projects." The Coalition for Green Capital (n.d.) defines green banks as "mission-driven institutions that use innovative financing to accelerate the transition to clean energy and fight climate change."

II. Background: Scaling Up Green Investment and Limits to Project-Based Mobilization of Private Capital[3]

Emerging markets and developing economies need enormous investment for climate mitigation and adaptation; for better and more inclusive economic, social, and ecological conditions; and to achieve the SDGs. ADB (2017) estimates that developing Asian economies need $1.7 trillion a year in climate-adjusted infrastructure investment in transportation, power, water and sanitation, and telecommunications. The United Nations Economic and Social Commission for Asia and the Pacific (UNESCAP 2019) estimates that an additional annual investment of $1.5 trillion is required to attain the SDGs by 2030 and end poverty and hunger; provide   sic health care, quality education, enabling infrastructure, and clean energy for all; and for climate action and living in harmony with nature (Figures 1 and 2). The COVID-19 pandemic has widened the financing gap substantially.[3]

The picture is bleak for international private capital flows to emerging and developing economies to finance climate action and the SDGs. Currently, a large portion of savings in these economies is invested—often at low or negative returns—in financial centers in advanced countries (Volz and Schoenmaker 2022). These capital exports are often channeled back to the economies as high-yielding, short-term debt or portfolio investment, which increases financial vulnerability. In past decades, many such economies, particularly in Asia and the Pacific and the oil-producing Middle East, have been running sizable current account surpluses—which means they have been net capital exporters—and building up foreign currency reserves as well as overseas assets.

Figure 1: Annual Investment Requirements for Asia and the Pacific, 2016–2030

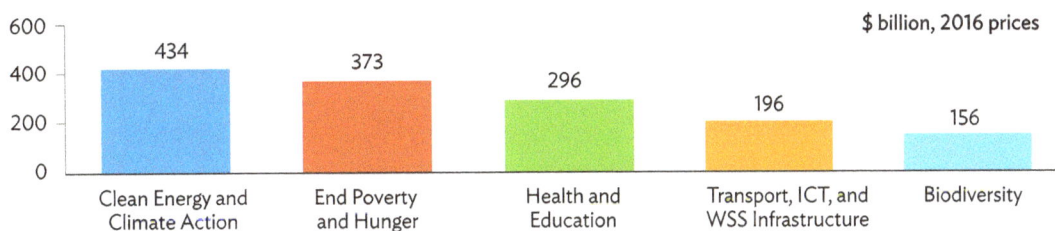

$ billion, 2016 prices

Clean Energy and Climate Action	434
End Poverty and Hunger	373
Health and Education	296
Transport, ICT, and WSS Infrastructure	196
Biodiversity	156

ICT = information and communications technology, WSS = water, sanitation and safe water.

Source: United Nations Economic and Social Commission for Asia and the Pacific (UNESCAP). 2019. Economic and Social Survey of Asia and the Pacific 2019: Ambitions Beyond Growth. Bangkok: UNESCAP.

---

[3]   This section draws on Volz and Schoenmaker (2022).

Figure 2: Annual Average Investment Gap in Transport, Information and Communications Technology, and Water and Sanitation Infrastructure, 2016–2030 (% of GDP)

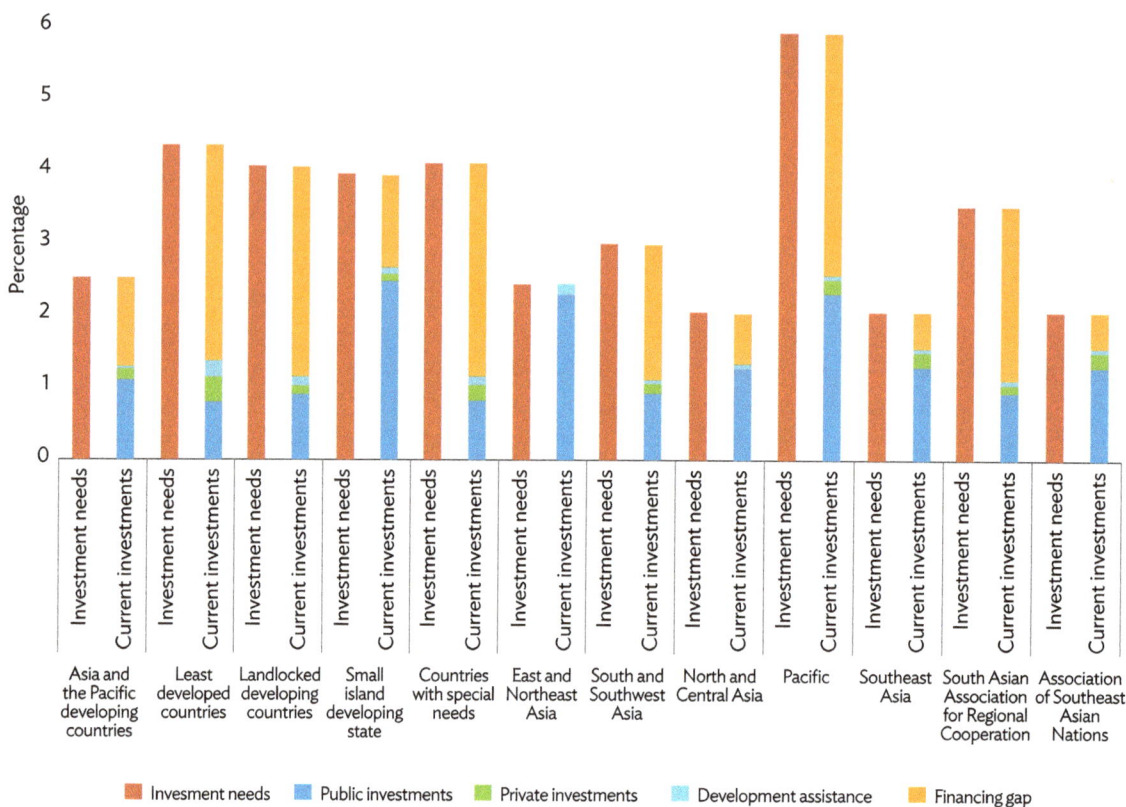

GDP = gross domestic product.

Source: United Nations Economic and Social Commission for Asia and the Pacific (UNESCAP). 2019. Economic and Social Survey of Asia and the Pacific 2019: Ambitions Beyond Growth. Bangkok: UNESCAP.

Between 2000 and 2021, emerging markets and developing economies, excluding the People's Republic of China (PRC) accumulated current account surpluses of $892 billion ($4.8 trillion including the PRC) (Volz and Schoenmaker 2022). These are only net capital exports; gross capital exports are much larger. In other words, while capital should be flowing from advanced countries, where it is abundant, to developing economies, where investment needs are much larger, aggregate capital flows are going in the other direction—they are flowing "uphill." Even in countries that are net capital importers (including most countries in Sub-Saharan Africa), significant amounts of domestic savings are invested abroad in safe, hard-currency assets, instead of the local economy.

The successful implementation of low-emission development strategies and national adaptation plans or national adaptation programs of action can only be achieved if domestic resource mobilization is strengthened. Efforts need to be reinforced to strengthen domestic financial resource mobilization for scaling up local climate-friendly, sustainable investments and reducing capital exports from developing to advanced economies.

Developing countries may export capital for many reasons, including a desire to build up foreign exchange reserves to build buffers and cushion against shocks, repayment of old debt, a diversification of investments, domestic financial and macroeconomic instability, political instability, and illicit flows. A key problem, however, is a lack of long-term investment opportunities at home due to underdeveloped capital markets. For addressing the climate investment and SDG financing gap, mobilizing domestic financial resources through the local banking system and capital markets and channeling them into domestic investments will be crucial. As discussed in Section 5, public financial institutions can play a critical role in this.

Likewise, better ways need to be found to attract patient private capital from abroad. Attempts to date to lure private capital at scale into emerging markets and developing economies have not been effective (Volz and Schoenmaker 2022). The "billions to trillions" agenda—the attempt to leverage private sector capital through project-based blended finance approaches—has not been successful. The track record of project-based "mobilization" or "de-risking" to leverage small amounts of public money to achieve trillion-dollar transformations is poor, especially in poorer countries (e.g., Attridge and Engen 2019). As Kenny (2022) puts it: "The idea you can use a little bit of public money to bring to life a vast array of private investment projects in infrastructure and services isn't just fiction, it is utter fantasy."

With the turning of the global financial cycle and sovereign debt problems mounting in many developing and emerging economies, private capital is now increasingly pulling out of developing and emerging economies. Rising rates in the major advanced economies make investments in the Global South comparatively less attractive. This reinforces the imperative for strengthening domestic financial resource mobilization and developing and implementing better approaches to mobilize international capital.

Leveraging private finance for climate and sustainable development through public banks ought to be part of the solution. Both MDBs and national development banks can use a tried-and-tested method of leveraging private sector finance for development: they can issue (sustainable) bonds and borrow from markets. MDBs especially can absorb large amounts of private domestic and international capital at cheap rates and on-lend it to developing country governments at low rates with longer tenors, or they can directly finance projects through equity or loans.[4] By doing so, they can also create safe, investable local currency assets that can attract domestic savings.[5] This is a much more effective way of leveraging private sector capital than project-based blended finance approaches. National development banks can, in principle, do the same, but for the time being they tend to be constrained by the higher cost of capital.

Section 5 discusses how to address this problem and how MDBs and other international development finance institutions can help unleash the potential of GIBs in countries of the Global South. Moreover, and very importantly, MDBs and national development banks can help overcome market failures and work with governments to create favorable framework conditions for green investments and help develop a project pipeline of investable projects, especially if they develop a strong expertise in green finance. Section 3 addresses this issue.

---

[4]   For instance, since 1944, the International Bank for Reconstruction and Development has leveraged the total paid-in capital of the members of the OECD Development Assistance Committee by a factor of 10 (Humphrey and Prizzon 2020).

[5]   Since the emerging market crises of the 1990s and early 2000s, concerted efforts have been made to develop local currency bond markets across emerging markets and developing economies. While these markets have grown considerably, helping to mitigate the currency mismatch problems that contributed to crises, the growing presence of foreign investors in the markets has created new risks for financial stability (Carstens and Shin 2019; Beirne, Renzhi, and Volz 2019).

III. The Case for Green Investment Banks

The case for public development banks in general, and GIBs in particular, rests on a pervasive market failure in private finance (Stiglitz 1994; Griffith-Jones, Attridge, and Gouett 2020). Perhaps most importantly, financial markets fail to properly account for positive and negative externalities. Private financial actors typically neglect to take negative externalities into account and incorporate them into their lending or investment decisions because they are not reflected in market prices. Likewise, they usually do not account for positive externalities since these do not create a revenue stream. This is a problem insofar as ignoring negative externalities in financing decisions leads to overinvestment in areas that harm societal welfare, while ignoring positive externalities leads to an undersupply of investment in activities that would enhance societal welfare. This is a serious problem for climate change and environmental degradation: since negative externalities of harmful emissions and pollution are not priced in (e.g., because of lack of or inadequate carbon prices), financial institutions continue to finance dirty economic activities that are worsening the climate and ecological crisis. At the same time, because the positive externalities of clean, low-carbon technologies are not priced in, the financial sector underfinances these technologies.

A second and related problem is the "short-termism" prevailing in financial markets: "the focus on short time horizons by both corporate managers and financial markets, prioritizing near-term shareholder interests over the long-term growth of the firm" (Mason 2016, 4). The pursuit of short-term profits leads to a suboptimal allocation of capital because longer-term benefits and risks are not properly accounted for. This is a severe problem in the context of environmental degradation and climate change, where the costs of harmful economic behavior often materialize in the medium or longer term. Mark Carney (2015), while serving as Governor of the Bank of England, has famously termed this as the "tragedy of the horizons."[6] Moreover, except for more mature markets, financial markets also tend to undersupply long-term credit because financial institutions are unable to internalize the full benefits of monitoring their debtors. Long-term (or patient) financing is thus scarce and expensive.

A third problem is that private financial markets tend to exclude riskier borrowers because of information asymmetries (Stiglitz and Weiss 1981, Stiglitz 1994). Because the information needed to assess risks is imperfect and costly to obtain—and thus beyond the reach of smaller businesses—it may be rational for commercial financial institutions to exclude micro, small, and medium-sized enterprises (MSMEs) and poorer households from financial services altogether or charge (often prohibitively) high rates. Climate change aggravates the problem: MSMEs and

---

[6] In Carney's words (2015, 3): "the catastrophic impacts of climate change will be felt beyond the traditional horizons of most actors – imposing a cost on future generations that the current generation has no direct incentive to fix."

poorer households are disproportionately exposed to climate risks and impacts, which worsens their risk profile even more and makes lending to them even less attractive (Volz et al. 2020). Also, both real economy and financial sector policies designed to advance the transition to a green, low-carbon economy can have unintended consequences for MSMEs (Volz and Knaack 2023). New environmental standards requiring businesses to adopt clean technology may threaten the survival of MSMEs unable to afford such investment or provide evidence of their "green credentials" (e.g., through sustainability assessment by third parties).

A fourth problem is that commercial financial institutions tend to shy away from high-risk investments with uncertain returns such as new technologies and the financing of innovative start-ups.[7] For instance, the development of renewable energy technologies would not have been possible without significant public investment. Moreover, the mass-market adoption of innovative technologies (such as renewables) may be difficult if costs are initially too high for commercial use and production at scale is needed to bend the cost curve.

As Griffith-Jones Attridge and Gouett (2020) highlight, public development banks can help overcome these market failures and play a key role in financing the structural transformation to sustainable development. Financially, these banks need to operate sustainably, but they are mission-oriented institutions with an explicit developmental mandate that need not generate high returns for their shareholders. In particular, equipped with a dedicated mandate to finance a green and just transition, green investment banks can accelerate adoption of clean, low-carbon technologies by reducing real and perceived risk and increasing the number of transactions in markets for new technologies.

Of particular importance is their role in providing long-term funding at affordable rates. The financing of low-carbon and climate-resilient infrastructure typically requires large upfront investment, while the payback period is long. Importantly, infrastructure projects typically do not generate positive cash flows in the early phases and are often characterized by high credit risk. The financing of many climate adaptation and mitigation projects is therefore often not attractive for commercial lenders. Long-maturity financing thus tends to be a big challenge for many developing economies with shallow capital markets and increasingly stringent banking regulations. If long-maturity finance is available, it is often prohibitively expensive. With government support, public development banks can provide longer-term finance. Indeed, over 50% of national development bank loans extend over 10 years (Griffith-Jones 2020). Importantly, public development banks can play a role in deepening local capital markets by issuing longer-term local currency bonds and use the proceeds to provide affordable and long-term finance for green investment. By doing so, they can help leverage scarce public resources. Because of a different capital and funding structure and their ability to provide patient, long-term committed finance, they can play a key role in fostering real innovation and entrepreneurship. They can do so by funding new sectors or cross cutting sectorial programs with high uncertainty and showcase the viability of certain green investments.

---

[7]   Venture capital firms do invest in high-risk start-ups that may generate breakthrough technologies and high returns, but only a few (usually advanced) economies have a flourishing venture capital ecosystem, and where they exist, incentives to invest in technologies that generate high positive externalities tend to be small.

Last but not least, public development banks can provide counter-cyclical finance. While private banks and other financial institutions tend to reduce their lending and investment during economic downturns—which then reinforces economic contraction—public development banks typically extend their engagement in times of crisis, as was evidenced after the 2008 financial crisis and during the COVID-19 crises (Griffith-Jones 2022). Given the dismal economic outlook in wide parts of the world and the urgency to invest in climate action, the need is great for public development banks in general, and GIBs in particular, to scale up funding for the green transition.

GIBs can help overcome investment barriers by using targeted approaches and tailored financial structuring to address the lack of suitable low-carbon climate-resilient investments with attributes sought by private investors, for instance through aggregation of small-scale investments. They can also address the shortage of objective information, data, and skills to assess transactions and underlying risks. GIBs can (and do) work with market participants to increase supply and demand for profitable low-carbon investments by decreasing risks, increasing market transparency, and improving investors' (and lenders') understanding of low-carbon investments. Moreover, GIBs can work with governments to create favorable framework conditions for green investments and help develop a project pipeline of green investable projects.

GIBs can be critical in transforming markets. They typically aim to demonstrate the profitability of low-carbon investments to accelerate market development and then move on to other investments where they can improve the risk-return profile and attract private investment. GIBs are better placed to play this role than traditional government programs—which may be less flexible and less familiar with markets—and private companies, which face competitive pressures. By dispersing information, sharing expertise, and demonstrating the profitability of green investments, GIBs can help reduce financing costs more quickly. They can also help project developers and investors adopt impact metrics to track progress on national climate and sustainability targets.

IV. Key Considerations in the Development of a Green Investment Bank

Currently, 522 subnational, national, regional, and global public development banks operate across the world (AFD 2022). Only a few of them, however, have an explicitly green mandate (Smallridge et al. 2013, AFD 2022). Moreover, most of them have been slow to align their operations and portfolios with the imperatives of the impending climate and ecological crisis.

The actual number of GIBs and GIB-like entities in operation is still small (Table 1; OECD 2015, 2017). Given the enormous investment needs in the green transformation, the rationale is strong for either transforming existing public development banks (both MDBs and national development banks) into GIBs or creating entirely new institutions. The former can be achieved by updating the mandates of public development banks to focus on a just, net-zero transition and possibly link this with a capital increase. New GIBs can be capitalized through governments, central banks, MDBs/development finance institutions, and global funds such as the Green Climate Fund, the Global Environment Facility, or the Climate Investment Funds.

Table 1: Green Investment Banks and Green Investment Bank-Like Entities in Operation

Green Investment Bank	Country	Established	Mission	Assets[a] ($ million)
Rhode Island Infrastructure Bank (formerly Water Finance Agency)	Rhode Island, US	1989/2015	Supports and invests in the state's infrastructure, businesses, and homeowners through the issuance of bonds, originating loans, and making grants, and the engagement with and mobilization of sources of public and private capital. Leverages capital in a revolving fund to offer innovative financing for an array of infrastructure-based projects including water and wastewater road and bridge energy efficiency and renewable energy brownfield remediation to improve the state's infrastructure, create jobs, promote economic development and enhance the environment.	1,623
New York Energy Efficiency Corporation	New York, US	2011	Provides loans for energy efficiency and clean energy projects in New York City and throughout the northeast and mid-Atlantic regions.	50

continued on next page

Table 1 *continued*

Green Investment Bank	Country	Established	Mission	Assets[a] ($ million)
Connecticut Green Bank (formerly Connecticut Clean Energy Fund)	Connecticut, US	2011	Supports the governor's and legislature's energy strategy to achieve cleaner, less expensive, and more reliable sources of energy while creating jobs and supporting local economic development. Works with private-sector investors to create low-cost, long-term sustainable financing to maximize the use of public funds.	258
California Lending for Energy and Environmental Needs Center (situated within California Infrastructure and Economic Development Bank)	California, US	2014	Provides low-cost direct public financing to local governments and nonprofits sponsored by public agencies to help meet the state's goals for greenhouse gas reduction, water conservation, and environmental preservation.	100
Green Energy Market Securitization (Hawaii Green Infrastructure Authority)	Hawaii, US	2014	Provides innovative financing products that bring clean energy technologies to Hawaii ratepayers, particularly underserved ratepayers.	148
Montgomery County Green Bank	Maryland, US	2015	Dedicated to accelerating energy efficiency, renewable energy, and clean energy investment in Montgomery County, Maryland. Partners with the private sector to provide more affordable and flexible financing options for county residents and businesses for clean energy and climate-resilient projects.	24
The Climate Access Fund	Maryland, US	2017	Aims to reduce the energy burden of low-income households through access to discounted clean energy. Offers attractive financial products to solar developers who offer discounted community solar rates to low- to moderate-income and disadvantaged households. Advocates for clean energy policies that benefit lower-income and disadvantaged communities.	...
Colorado Clean Energy Fund	Colorado, US	2018	Provides access to capital for clean energy by offering a portfolio of loan products to help residential, commercial, industrial, agricultural, municipal, affordable housing and nonprofit borrowers break down barriers of clean energy adoption.	...

continued on next page

Table 1 *continued*

Green Investment Bank	Country	Established	Mission	Assets[a] ($ million)
DC Green Bank	Washington, DC, US	2018	Provides access to capital to grow a clean economy and to develop a more equitable, resilient, and sustainable Washington, DC by offering innovative financing solutions that prioritize making the clean economy inclusive and affordable for all city residents, businesses, and community institutions. Focuses its investments on solar energy, greener and more efficient buildings, infrastructure resilience, and transportation electrification.	26
Malaysian Green Technology and Climate Change Centre	Malaysia	2010	Provides loan guarantees and subsidies to encourage private banks to finance green projects.	...
UK Green Investment Bank[b]	United Kingdom	2012	Was mandated to accelerate the UK's transition to a greener, stronger economy by investing in green projects and mobilizing private finance into the green energy sector.	n/a
Clean Energy Finance Corporation	Australia	2012	Aims to cut emissions by investing $10 billion on behalf of the government in agriculture, cleantech innovation, energy generation and storage. Collaborates with investors, innovators and industry leaders to spur substantial new investment where it will have the greatest impact.	4,391
Green Fund	Japan	2013	Provides equity and mezzanine investments that attract further capital from private resources to solidify the business case of small to large scale clean energy projects.	...
Technology Fund	Switzerland	2014	Provides loan guarantees to banks and other suitable lenders for loans to Swiss companies whose novel products contribute to a sustainable reduction in greenhouse gas emissions.	...
New Zealand Green Investment Finance	New Zealand	2019	Seeks to accelerate and facilitate investment in emissions reductions in New Zealand. Invest on a commercial basis and seeks to crowd-in private capital.	64

... = not available.

[a] Total assets for 2021 or latest year available.

[b] The UK Green Investment Bank was privatized in 2017 and ceased to exist as an independent institution.

Source: Compiled by author drawing from the Global Database on Public Development Banks and Development Financing Institutions. Xu, J., R. Marodon, X. Ru, X. Ren, and X. Wu. 2021. What are Public Development Banks and Development Financing Institutions? Qualification Criteria, Stylized Facts and Development Trends. China Economic Quarterly International. 1 (4). pp. 271–294 (updated version: November 2022); and OECD Policy Perspectives: Green Investment Banks, December 2015.

As OECD (2016) highlights, the "greening" of existing institutions may be preferable to creating new GIBs from scratch, given sufficient institutional and political support for this transition. Establishing a new financing institution requires both capital (political and financial) and time. It can thus be constructive and faster to work with existing institutions. Existing national development banks tend to be much larger than even the largest GIBs. Also, some national development banks, such as Germany's KfW, have already developed large green portfolios. As noted, several MDBs have been seeking to transform themselves into GIBs or "climate banks"—this could be replicated at the national (or subnational) level. Building on the existing capacities of national development banks updating their mandates with explicit green targets and making a concerted effort to build the specific expertise to finance the green transformation may thus be a sensible way forward. But even when an existing national development bank will not be transformed into a full-fledged GIB, it will be critical to ensure that all such banks (as well as MDBs) fully align their operations and portfolios with the climate goals and the SDGs. In this respect, the United Nations Development Programme, in collaboration with the Finance in Common Secretariat, recently put forward recommendations for enhancing the role of public development banks in scaling up sustainable finance (Box 1).

Box 1: Enhancing the Role of Public Development Banks in Scaling Up Sustainable Finance

1. Recommendations to improve public development banks' mandates, strategies, and governance aligned to Sustainable Development Goals

In general, the results of the interviews and survey demonstrated a common understanding and agreement regarding the importance of aligning with the Sustainable Development Goals (SDGs) and the Paris Agreement at a strategic and ambitious level, while signaling a range of important challenges, as well as good practices and opportunities including future support from partners in the development community.

Align public development banks' mandates and activities with the Paris Agreement and SDGs by providing them with the right incentives, shifting away from investments incompatible with a just and inclusive transition to sustainable, low-carbon, and resilient development trajectories. For example, climate finance now accounts for 20% of total commitments made by International Development Finance Club members on average. If public development banks were to commit to a similar ratio, they could extend more than $500 billion of climate finance per year and mobilize much more through the private sector.

Pursue an integrated approach to net impact, combining negative screening with a positive assessment of impact rather than having many separate processes towards achieving SDGs, both at a strategic and project level. The interdependence between the SDGs is still a particularly difficult issue for public development banks. Greater awareness plus new tools to manage potential trade-offs between equality, gender, poverty, unemployment, climate, and environment are important. The huge challenges countries face, exacerbated by COVID-19, make it even more important to address potential trade-offs and ensure that a focus on vital issues like gender-based violence is not lost in big-picture debates on the SDGs.

continued on next page

Box 1 *continued*

Enhance alignment of strategies between the national/subnational government and public development banks. This can include increased dialogue between public development banks and national authorities through engagement with Integrated National Financing Frameworks, financing strategies, and dialogue platforms to enable and strengthen these banks' specific inputs into national financing and strategy development. In addition, this can help ministries of finance, environment, and development to shape well-aligned national strategies that take each perspective into account.

Ensure sufficient training and support for public development bank board members. This goes particularly for non-executives, who may change frequently due to political changes, and for staff more generally, so they can understand the drivers of change and support strategic reforms. Comprehensive training, capacity development measures, and clear support from the leadership are required, alongside other key changes.

2. Recommendations to improve lending, guarantees, pricing and currency risk

Enable public development banks by providing them with lower-cost finance, given that they are trying to support development objectives, but often through recipients that are heavily focused on short-term survival. At the moment, there is often no difference between the costs of "normal" funding and sustainable loans, meaning there is not much incentive for recipients to take sustainable loans if reporting or other requirements are more demanding. Since public development banks do not have individual customer deposits as a source of low-cost financing, they can be at a disadvantage compared to commercial banks. Furthermore, engagement with credit rating agencies may be important so that they do not reduce a public development bank rating as it aligns with SDGs, which would increase the banks' cost of capital.

Support for longer-term finance in addition to lowering the cost, because the long-term investments and longer-term payoffs that can be associated with SDG alignment need to be matched by longer-term funding to help the business case. Too often the funding is too short-term.

Support public development banks in dealing with currency risk when receiving support in US dollars or other international currencies but lending in local currency. Most public development banks, and especially smaller national or subnational public development banks in developing countries, cannot afford to hedge the currency risk when they receive support in US dollars from development partners but have to lend to national recipients in local currency. It is vital for the G20 and others to cover or reduce the costs of this currency risk given public development banks with projects in one country cannot diversify it.

Enable access to affordable experts to provide technical assistance to enhance public development bank capacity and that of project partners, whether from domestic or international sources.

3. Recommendations to improve data, measurement, impact, and taxonomies

Develop clear definitions and taxonomies on common impact measurement standards that link directly to the desired outcomes. These are preconditions to support SDG-aligned projects and prevent greenwashing and social investment washing. A strong push on a limited set of standards that can be implemented without great cost would make lending policy much simpler.

continued on next page

Box 1 *continued*

Promote harmonized taxonomies in particular to make more progress on structuring asset classes because climate and social investment finance can scale if financial actors can create transparent asset classes into which people can invest. The asset classes should be well-designed so that they do not negatively impact other SDG targets and transparently deliver a positive impact.

Support improved data and reporting for public development banks and clients, through technical assistance and direct support to priority sectors to improve data and reporting, particularly on gender. This is also important because collecting additional data to track alignment with SDGs can raise costs.

4. Recommendations to promote effective collaboration and international support

Focus on issues that will attract the private sector to the field, boost collaboration, and potentially help evolve public development bank business models where needed for the future. One element is harmonized taxonomies (as above). In addition, bringing the private sector—including commercial banks, investment funds, the pension and insurance sector—and public development banks together more generally can help expand public development bank impact, in addition to closer links to the government and public sector actions outlined above.

Enhance commitment from the development community, including the G20, to support the mobilization of public development banks and private finance even more, given limited government budgets badly affected by the pandemic. To achieve the SDGs by 2030, and address pandemic recovery and a just transition, will be too difficult from fiscal space alone. So, the G20 and other international groups, including the multilateral development banks, could continue to boost the profile and need for engagement with public development banks and coordinate amongst themselves to reduce overlap and ensure maximum impact.

Ensure it is simpler to deploy funds provided by international partners and that consistent financing operates alongside the flexibility to fund new and innovative approaches. For some funds, cumbersome accountability mechanisms discourage the use of facilities. In addition, some public development banks find that funding does not last long enough to achieve results, while others want more rapid transfers of resources to emerging priorities and innovative approaches.

Apply more emphasis on subnational capacity and the ability to focus on a local level. Building on strong knowledge of local market stakeholders, public development banks, and subnational development banks can play a critical role in bridging the subnational financial gap. This local knowledge can relate to key gaps for intervention in different parts of a country and help external investors not duplicate existing initiatives or repeat past mistakes. It can also create the delivery partnerships that will ensure a project is successful, including engaging local stakeholders, especially women, and those who may not traditionally have a voice in the development process. Finally, there can be benefits for data project monitoring and evaluation.

Source: Adapted from Finance in Common and United Nations Development Programme. 2022. Joint Report: The Role of Public Development Banks in Scaling Sustainable Financing. New York: United Nations Development Programme.

However, valid reasons exist for establishing new, dedicated GIBs. Reforming existing national development banks may be fraught with political problems and resistance from current structures. Leadership and staff need to be committed to the mission of financing a green transition and need to have relevant expertise in sustainable finance and the green economy, something that cannot be taken for granted among the staff of "old"/conventional national development banks.

Many national development banks have thus far not played meaningful roles in mobilizing green investment and have broader developmental agendas—rewiring such institutions, implementing new mandates and structures, and building the relevant expertise may, in some cases, be more cumbersome than establishing an entirely new institution. Indeed, the majority of public development banks have already quite specific mandates (Figure 3). These can certainly be "greened," but it may be challenging to turn a public development bank focused on the financing of MSMEs into a GIB that will do large-scale (green) infrastructure finance. Moreover, financing the green transition requires new approaches, something that older institutions may find difficult to adapt to. Table 2 reviews relevant considerations.

Figure 3: Percentage of Assets of Public Development Banks by Mandate, 2022

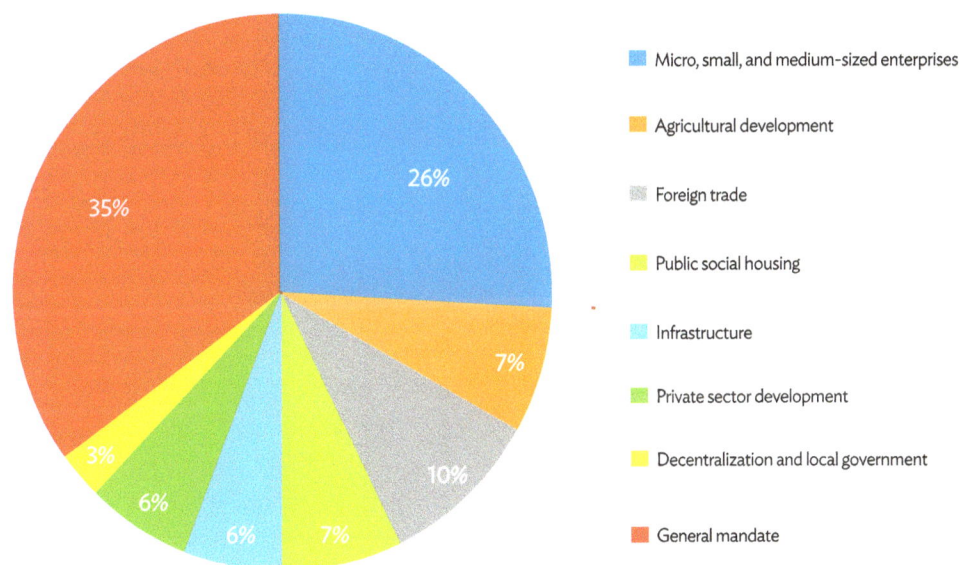

Legend:
- Micro, small, and medium-sized enterprises
- Agricultural development
- Foreign trade
- Public social housing
- Infrastructure
- Private sector development
- Decentralization and local government
- General mandate

Source: Compiled with data from AFD (2022).

Table 2: Greening an Existing National Development Bank vs. Creating a New Green Investment Bank

Costs: Establishing a new institution likely involves more time and cost than greening an existing institution and may be viewed as expanding bureaucracy or creating duplicative government services.

Independence and authority: Creating a new green investment bank (GIB) with an independent status can provide flexibility to experiment, innovate, and adapt to market developments. It can also shield the institution from day-to-day political interference.

Mandate and culture: Many national development banks lack a clear mandate to promote national climate change mitigation. Such banks may support renewable energy projects while also financing fossil fuel projects in parallel. In contrast, GIBs focus exclusively on green investment and face fewer competing agendas.

Financing approaches: The types of preferred financing approaches vary across GIBs, national development banks and multilateral development banks. GIBs tend to orient more toward accelerating risk-taking by investors through demonstration, co-investment, and sharing risks with investors using guarantees and other risk mitigants.

Scale: The low-carbon investment portfolios of some national development banks are larger than those of even the largest GIB. If national development banks mainstream green investment throughout their portfolios, they may be able to mobilize low-carbon, climate-resilient infrastructure at much greater scale than GIBs. However, if GIBs were able to significantly augment their current capitalization by securing funds from other sources (e.g., the Green Climate Fund), the scale advantage held by national development banks could diminish.

Benefits of centralizing green bank functions in one institution: An alternative to "greening" a single institution such as a national development bank is to strengthen and expand a green investment program already housed in government agencies and institutions. Interventions undertaken by some programs and institutions, such as transaction structuring and co-investing, require different skills than providing subsidies and concessional lending. In addition, such interventions may cover a number of unrelated sectors. As a result, bringing these functions together in the same institution may not yield efficiency gains. However, efficiency gains could result from bringing together transactional expertise in similar technologies, projects and business models, particularly if staff have the financial and sector knowledge to undertake a range of interventions. Consolidation of programs and related outreach would also facilitate information sharing with retail and commercial customers and other investors.

Source: Adapted from OECD (2016).

Whether established from scratch or developed out of an existing national development bank, certain conditions need to be met for GIBs to operate well and unleash their potential. Most importantly, GIBs can only operate effectively if the country has a clear development strategy focused on green (and just) transition and if policy frameworks are enabling, not blocking green investments. In fact, through its operations on the ground, GIBs can play a key role in helping policymakers to create better enabling environments for low-carbon, climate-resilient projects and the formulation and achievement of nationally determined contributions and national adaptation plans. They can do this by providing policy advice and lending technical expertise in the green economy to the government. Of course, stable macroeconomic conditions are also crucial.

Setting up a new GIB requires capital. Various national financial sources (including government appropriations, utility bill charges or carbon tax revenues, and capital injection by the central bank) can be used to capitalize a GIB (OECD 2016), but—as discussed in the next section—there may be good reasons to also tap international sources (MDBs/development finance institutions, global funds). In principle, governments could also invite private investors to contribute capital.

Different forms of governance are possible. GIBs can be independent or quasi-independent of government or exist as independent units or funds operating within the government (OECD 2016). What is critical is that they have a focused mandate with a clear mission for financing low-carbon climate-resilient investment or a green economy more broadly. Equally important is that GIBs are accountable, and that their performance is measured against clearly specified key performance indicators. As OECD (2016) highlights, GIBs' public reporting on their performance should include transparent calculation methodologies to build credibility.

In principle, GIBs should focus on financing activities that generate positive externalities and that are not financed by commercial financial institutions, or only at high rates. In other words, GIBs should primarily finance transactions that would not occur without their involvement (OECD 2016). Types of GIB interventions (Figure 4), include direct financing of investments, provision of risk-mitigating credit enhancements, and various transaction enablers. GIBs can use different investment instruments and funds, including loans, equity, mezzanine finance, investment funds, bonds, structured notes, and grants (Figure 5).

Figure 4: Types of Green Investment Bank Interventions

Directly finance investment in low-carbon and climate-resilient infrastructure using a range of instruments and funds, including senior and subordinate loans, bond-based financing, and equity.

Provide risk-mitigating credit enhancements such as loan loss reserves and guarantees to reduce risks for private sector lenders.

Encourage adoption of repayment mechanisms such as on-bill finance, which facilitates repayment through existing utility bills and reduces default risk for lenders.

Transaction enablers such as warehousing and securitization increase the flow of institutional capital by bundling small-scale projects to achieve scale and reduce transaction costs.

Source: Adapted from OECD (2016).

Figure 5: Investment Instruments and Funds Used by Green Investment Banks

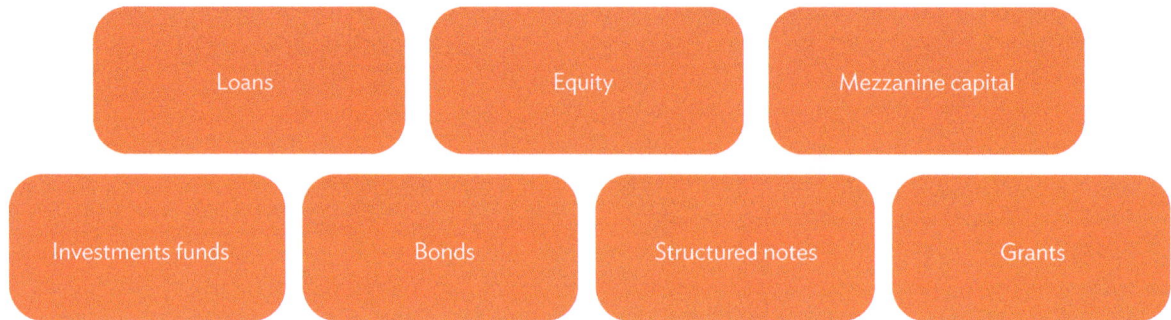

Loans	Equity	Mezzanine capital

Investments funds	Bonds	Structured notes	Grants

Source: Adapted from OECD (2016).

V. How Can Development Finance Institutions Support Green Investment Banks in the Global South?

International development finance institutions (meaning multilateral institutions or institutions owned by high-income countries) can support the establishment of new GIBs and help existing national development banks reinvent themselves as GIBs and play a larger role in climate and SDG finance. They can do this in two ways: (i) by offering technical assistance to help the build-up of strong governance structures and expertise in financing green infrastructure and projects; and (ii) by providing capital or credit enhancements to enable GIBs to obtain higher ratings to refinance themselves at more favorable conditions or by passing on concessionary financing to GIBs.

First, most development finance institutions have a wealth of experience in delivering technical assistance projects and capacity building for banking and financial management. Building on this, they can help existing national development banks build strong governance structures and sustainable finance expertise when reinventing themselves as GIBs; they can do the same when helping governments establish a brand-new GIB from scratch.

Second, development finance institutions can play a critical role in helping GIBs build a strong standing in capital markets which is reflected in a strong credit rating that will help improve GIB's ability to raise capital in markets at lower rates. This is critical. To build a green, low-carbon economy, a large upfront investment is needed. This constitutes a big problem for emerging and developing economies, which face a much higher cost of capital (Figure 6), a problem aggravated by their climate vulnerability (Buhr et al. 2018, Kling et al. 2018). For GIBs to catalyze financing for the green transition and effectively leverage the capital their shareholders provide, they need cheap refinancing. However, they face a serious obstacle: The funding cost of financial institutions in emerging and developing economies—including national development banks (and by implication also nationally owned GIBs)—are constrained by a sovereign ceiling effect which has a direct impact on their cost of capital (Almeida et al. 2017). The financing conditions of national development banks are effectively determined by the sovereign credit rating of the government that backs it. This is true for borrowing in local and international currency.

Figure 6: Cost of Capital for a Solar Photovoltaic Project, 2021

%

9%–13.5%

2.5%–5.5%

Advanced Economies and PRC   Emerging and Developing Economies

PRC = People's Republic of China.
Source: IEA 2022.

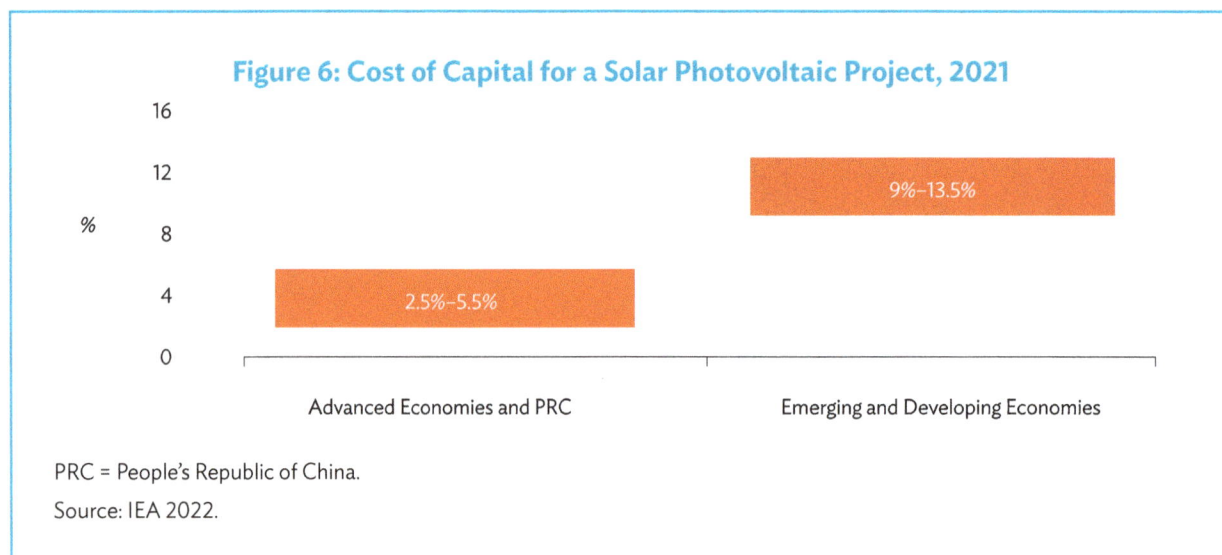

Since national development banks are usually fully government-owned, their credit risk cannot be better than that of the government. The government can always take out capital or force the national development bank to lend to the government if it gets into financial dire straits. The national development banks are rated under criteria for government-related entities (e.g., S&P Global 2015).[8] Often the ratings are equalized with those of the sovereign, notwithstanding that their standalone credit quality is usually lower than that of the sovereign (Table 3).[9] While institutions like Germany's KfW benefit from the AAA rating of the German government that allows it to issue debt at low cost, national development banks of developing countries face a much higher cost of capital due to lower credit ratings.[10] This impedes the part that nationally owned GIBs could assume in financing and accelerating the green transition.

International development finance institutions can help address the cost of capital problems of national development banks/GIBs in several ways. First, they can directly provide capital. To be meaningful for the GIB's credit rating and financing cost, however, the capital share would have to be significant—which means that the sovereign would have to give up full control of the GIB and share this with the development finance institution.[11] As is the case with MDBs, part of the development finance institution's contribution could be callable (or guarantee) capital. Besides the actual capital contribution, the involvement of the institution would also reassure capital markets of the high standards of governance of the GIB.

---

[8] The Development Bank of Southern Africa provides an example of how rating agencies look at national development banks.

[9] This may be considered a somewhat generous treatment as it assumes an almost certain likelihood to support the national development bank even if the sovereign itself is on the brink of default. Effectively, it is like rating callable capital for MDBs equally with the sovereign obligations of the government promising to stump up the callable capital in full and in time when asked to do so.

[10] Likewise, MDBs can borrow cheaply from international capital markets because they are backed by the guarantees of their highly-rated member governments (Nelson 2020).

[11] Bringing in subordinated capital via development finance institutions would not help.

Table 3: Ratings of Selected Public Development Banks and Sovereigns, as of November 2022

Public Development Bank	Country	Rating	Sovereign Rating
Asian Development Bank	Supranational	AAA	—
African Development Bank	Supranational	AAA	—
Asian Infrastructure Investment Bank	Supranational	AAA	—
European Bank for Reconstruction and Development	Supranational	AAA	—
Bank for Investment and Development of Vietnam	Viet Nam	Ba2	Ba2+
Export-Import Bank of Malaysia Berhad	Malaysia	A3	A3
Japan International Cooperation Agency	Japan	A+	A+
Korea Development Bank	Korea, Rep. of	AA	AA
Sarana Multi Infrastruktur	Indonesia	BBB	BBB
Development Bank of Southern Africa	South Africa	BB-	BB-
Banco Nacional de Desenvolvimento Econômico e Social	Brazil	BB-	BB-
KfW	Germany	AAA	AAA

— = not applicable.

Note: The ratings are for long-term foreign currency issuance by S&P Global, except for Bank for Investment and Development of Vietnam, EXIM Bank, and Housing and Urban Development Corporation, for which the ratings are from Moody's, and for Sarana Multi Infrastruktur, for which the ratings are from Fitch.

Source: Compiled by author.

An alternative that would allow the government to retain full ownership of the GIB would be likely that the development finance institution offers callable capital in exchange for seat(s) on the GIB board. This should lift the GIB's rating by one or two notches, compared to a situation without development finance institution involvement. This would be analogous to the treatment of callable capital at MDBs.

Second, and politically easier to arrange, development finance institutions can provide credit enhancement to national development banks/GIBs, for example by guaranteeing the bonds they issue. The issuer credit rating would remain low and unchanged. However, the bond issue would benefit from the guarantor's (i.e., the development finance institution's) higher ratings. That is what matters for the cost of funding.

Third, it is politically and operationally much easier for international development finance institutions to issue bonds themselves (benefiting from their high rating) and then on-lend at AAA conditions plus a small margin to nationally owned GIBs. This already happens in some cases with national development banks. The problem, however, is that this approach would not provide the leverage that would be created under the first two options: the national GIBs would not be able to act as multipliers and issue debt themselves. The first two options would thus be preferable.

The existing instruments of major MDBs could be used for all three options. For instance, the ADB could use established instruments such as policy-based loans and sovereign financial intermediation loans. Policy-based loans provide general budget support to public sector borrowers, helping countries that are facing a financing gap in their annual budget. It is disbursed only when the borrower completes policy reforms or actions that have been agreed with ADB. Under financial intermediation loans (FILs), the borrower onlends ADB funds to eligible financial intermediaries, like local banks or other financial institutions. These then provide smaller loans at sub-lenders' own credit risk to sub-borrowers (e.g., small and medium-sized enterprises). Such loans can be targeted to support the operations of new GIBs or the transformation of existing institutions and become important instruments to enhance the low-cost funding options of GIBs.

FILs can provide nascent GIBs access to lower-cost loans. In the case of ADB, FILs are extended on the condition that financial intermediation lending activities must be consistent with ADB's overall strategy for financial sector development in developing member countries, as reflected in the country strategy and program. Such loans should contribute to the establishment of financial institutions and systems that can raise and allocate resources in developing member countries efficiently and sustainably. FILs may be considered when there is effective demand for credit by potential sub-borrowers and the demand cannot be efficiently met through the domestic financial system due to market failure or structural problems, which are expected to be resolved through policy and institutional reforms, capacity building, and/or improvements in the macroeconomic environment over time.[12] Box 2 explains ADB's financial intermediation loans in Sri Lanka to fund good renewable energy projects.

---

[12]   The Operations Manual Bank Policies on ADB's Financial Intermediation Loans provide information on the use of funds for FILs: Para 11. FILs can finance subprojects for the production of and trade in goods and services and the development of housing and infrastructure. Subprojects are usually undertaken by the private sector, although public sector subprojects can be considered depending on the sector and country situation. Subprojects must meet criteria stipulated and defined by ADB, including financial and economic viability and positive developmental impact. Subprojects should also comply with the requirements of social and environmental legislation and regulations of the DMC, as well as conform to ADB's safeguard policies. Sub-borrowers must have acceptable debt/equity ratios (in the case of larger small- and medium-sized enterprise or other companies) and the capacity to repay the sub-loan, and to provide their own funds in cash or other assets acceptable to ADB to cover part of the total subproject cost.
Para 12. ADB generally does not support directed credit schemes, as these involve the allocation of resources outside market-based mechanisms, which can lead to economic inefficiencies. However, ADB may target FILs at specific types of subproject beneficiaries, such as (but not limited to) microenterprises, small- and medium-sized or export-oriented enterprises, women entrepreneurs, low-income groups, and private infrastructure projects. Such targeting would be done to promote certain development objectives in line with a DMC's poverty reduction and economic growth strategies, as reflected in the country strategy and program. However, beneficiaries should be defined broadly enough to enable financial intermediaries to make prudent lending decisions based on commercial considerations. Such FILs should be accompanied by programs and policy reforms that address underlying market imperfections and institutional problems inhibiting market-based credit flows to targeted groups, sectors, or regions.
Para 13. For each FIL, ADB usually specifies, on a case-by-case basis, the maximum amount of eligible subloans to ensure a reasonable number of subprojects taking into consideration project objectives.

**Box 2: ADB's Financial Intermediation Loans on Sri Lanka
for Renewable Energy Project**

In September 2017, the Asian Development Bank approved the Rooftop Solar Power Generation Project in Sri Lanka which aims to help the government establish a lending facility to support rooftop solar financing in line with its goal of increasing solar photovoltaic capacity to 200 megawatts (MW) by 2020 and 1,000 MW by 2025. The project provides a credit line through the Ministry of Finance to participating financial institutions, including both public and private sector banks, for the installation of rooftop solar photovoltaic power generation systems. Technical assistance was provided to establish technical guidelines and standards; assist in the development of a viable subproject pipeline to catalyze market demand for funds; support credit line implementation review, monitoring, and reporting; and conduct capacity building and awareness training and workshops for stakeholders.

By the end of 2019, about 2,081 subprojects have been approved amounting to 23.5 megawatts of total solar photovoltaic installations. Moreover, technical verification post-installation was supported. A detailed research study on large-scale photovoltaic integration to the grid was also conducted.

In 2020, the project received an additional financing of $250,000 from the Clean Energy Fund under the Clean Energy Financing Partnership Facility. By project completion, renewable energy capacity of 60 MW is expected to be developed with an estimated gross power generation of 94.6 gigawatt-hours per year. The project will also contribute the reduction of Sri Lanka's greenhouse gas emissions by 66,800 tons of carbon dioxide equivalent annually.

Source: ADB. Sri Lanka: Rooftop Solar Power Generation Project (3571-SRI). Manila.

VI. Case Studies

As noted, the actual number of GIBs in operation remains very small (Table 1). Besides a number of subnational GIBs in the United States, to date, the United Kingdom's (UK) Green Investment Bank is the only GIB established by a national government. But several GIB-like entities also operate. After providing an overview of the Connecticut Green Bank and the UK GIB, this section briefly discusses two Asian GIB-like entities: Malaysia's Green Technology Financing Scheme and Japan's Green Fund and Green Innovation Fund.

United States Connecticut Green Bank

The Connecticut Green Bank, established in July 2011, is the first green bank in the United States. It supports the governor's and legislature's energy strategy to achieve cleaner, less expensive, and more reliable sources of energy while creating jobs and supporting local economic development. The organization evolved from the Connecticut Clean Energy Fund, which was given a broader mandate in 2011 to become the Connecticut Green Bank. The green bank model upended the government subsidy-driven approach to clean energy by working with private-sector investors to create low-cost, long-term sustainable financing to maximize the use of public funds. It continues to innovate, educate, and activate to accelerate the growth of green energy measures. The Green Bank has established 11 legally separate for-profit entities whose collective purpose is to administer Green Bank's clean energy programs.[13] The range of financial products is discussed in Box 3.

Since its inception, the Green Bank mobilized more than $2.26 billion of investment into the state's green economy, with a leverage ratio of $7.00 for every $1.00. The State of Connecticut has transferred $72.78 million of net assets to facilitate the creation of the Green Bank from the former Clean Energy Finance and Investment Authority (CEFIA) in 2011. The size of the lending of the Connecticut Bank has steadily increased from $10.7 million worth of promissory note loans since its establishment in 2011 to $91.9 million worth of program loans and solar lease notes as of 2021. Going through the pandemic, the size of the lending significantly increased by $6.255 million in 2021 from $85.682 million in 2020.[14]

---

[13] These are: CEFIA Holdings LLC, CT Solar Loan I LLC, CEFIA Solar Services, Inc., CT Solar Lease 2 LLC, CT Solar Lease 3 LLC, CGB Meridien Hydro LLC, SHREC ABS 1 LLC, SHREC Warehouse 1 LLC, CT Solar Lease 1 LLC, CGB C-PACE LLC, and CGB Green Liberty Notes LLC.

[14] Connecticut Green Bank, Annual Comprehensive Financial Report.

Box 3: Connecticut Green Bank Portfolio of Solutions, Products and Services

There are a range of financial products and services and technical assistance provided by the Connecticut Green Bank, namely, Home Solutions, Building Solutions, Investment Solutions, Contractor Solutions, and Community Solutions. Specific examples of these solutions are: Smart-E loans, Multi-Family Financing, Commercial Property Assessed Clean Energy (C-PACE), Green Liberty Notes & Bonds, Green Bank Capital Solutions, EV Charging Carbon Credits and Sustainable CT.

Smart E-Loans – a financing type under home solutions which can be availed through these range of sub-products: Home Energy Improvements, Energy Storage Solutions Batteries and Residential Solar Options. In particular, specific usage would include home performance and efficiency, heating and cooling, water heating, renewables, other related energy measures, and other solar energy options.

Multi-family Financing – a financing type under building solutions which caters to more than 5 units and can be availed through these products: Navigator Pre-development Plan (technical and professional services), Solar Power Purchase Agreements, Solar Roof Lease, Health and Safety Loan and Loans Improving Multifamily Efficiency for energy improvements.

C-PACE (Commercial Property Assessed Clean Energy) Financing – a type of financing under Building Solutions focused on providing solutions for commercial buildings of all types to access green upgrades to new and existing buildings. It can be accessed in various sub-products such as Retrofitting, New Construction, Solar Programs (e.g., Solar PPA, Solar Roof Lease, etc.) and energy storage products.

Green Liberty Bonds and Notes – a type of financing under investment solutions to finance existing programs with green bonds including Certified Climate Bonds. Green Liberty Notes are easy-to-purchase investment financial instruments through an online platform without a broker, with a minimum $100 minimum. Proceeds will help strengthen communities and combat climate change. Investments in the notes help finance programs that give zero-interest energy efficiency loans to small businesses, so they can reduce their energy costs and directly improve their bottom lines.

Green Bank Capital Solutions – under investment solutions, it catalyzes the green energy economy in Connecticut by providing access to project developers and others to capital to realize projects that support Connecticut's goals for clean energy deployment and energy efficiency, reduction of greenhouse gasses, improved public health outcomes, job creation and economic development. The Request for Proposals is open to technologies that have already proven to be commercially viable or have demonstrated clear potential for commercial viability through well-documented feasibility studies or pilot programs with clear evidence of a viable business model and path to sustainable impact.

Electric Vehicle charging carbon credits – under investment solutions, it has developed a methodology to quantify carbon reductions, now accredited by Verified Carbon Standard, allowing the Green Bank to provide third-party certified carbon offset credits. By accessing difficult-to-reach voluntary carbon trading markets and aggregating portfolios of electric vehicle charging stations through this new and innovative approach, the Green Bank can help monetize these credits and generate revenue.

Contractor Solutions – for contractors who need financing, they can avail various loan products covering home solutions, building solutions, and investment solutions.

Sustainable CT – a type of financing under Community Solution which supports wide-ranging sustainability initiatives throughout Connecticut and the Connecticut Green Bank to engage communities, drive investment in projects, and improve sustainability. The Green Bank provides programmatic support to help the municipality be more sustainable and earn certification.

Source: The Connecticut Green Bank (accessed 10 March 2023).

Having the biggest share in terms of consolidated revenues (Table 4), the Connecticut Green Bank derives its revenue from utility assessments, auction proceeds from the Regional Greenhouse Gas Initiative, grants, and interest income from Commercial Property Assessed Clean Energy (C-PACE) and program loans. SHREC ABS 1 LLC derives revenue from interest income and the sale of Solar Home Renewable Energy Certificates (SHRECs) to two Connecticut utilities for two tranches of approximately 14,000 rooftop photovoltaic (PV) systems. SHREC Warehouse 1 LLC obtains revenue from interest income and the sale of SHRECs to two Connecticut utilities for a tranche of approximately 4,800 PV systems. CEFIA Holdings LLC derives revenue from interest income from program loans as earned and the Sale of Solar Renewable Energy Certificates (SRECs) to third parties. In essence, much of the revenues of these units are derived from the program loans extended by the bank as part of their solutions portfolio and the sale of energy certificates.

Table 4: Share in Revenue of Entities under the Connecticut Green Bank

Entities under the Connecticut Green Bank	Included in CGB's Financial Reporting	Operating Revenues as of 30 June 2022 ($ thousand)	Share ratio (%)
Connecticut Green Bank	Yes (Reporting Entity)	48,239	85.8
CGB Meriden Hydro LLC	Yes	0	0.0
SHREC ABS 1 LLC	Yes	4,360	7.8
SHREC Warehouse 1 LLC	Yes	1,980	3.5
CT Solar Lease 1 LLC	Yes	216	0.4
CT Solar Loan 1 LLC	Yes	67	0.1
CEFIA Holdings LLC	Yes	1,259	2.2
CEFIA Solar Services, Inc.	Yes	0	0.0
CGB Green Liberty Notes LLC	Yes	33	0.1
CGB C-PACE LLC	Yes	97	0.2
CT Solar Lease 2 LLC	No	0	0.0
CT Solar Lease 3 LLC	No	0	0.0
Total Revenues		**56,250**	**100.0**

C-PACE = Commercial Property Assessed Clean Energy, CEFIA = Clean Energy Finance and Investment Authority, CGB = Connecticut Green Bank, CT = Connecticut, SHREC = Solar Home Renewable Energy Certificates.

Note: CT Solar Lease 2 LLC and CT Solar Lease 3 LLC are not included in the financial reporting of the parent company, the Connecticut Green Bank since they have a separate set of financial statements.

Source: Connecticut Green Bank Fiscal Year 2022 Financial Statements.

Since its inception, the Connecticut Green Bank and its private investment partners have deployed over $2.2 billion in capital for clean energy projects across the state. Projects recorded through fiscal year 2022 show that for every $1 of public funds committed by the Connecticut Green Bank an additional $7.0 in private investment occurred in the economy (Table 5).

Table 5: Project Investments during Fiscal Years 2012–2022

Year	Total Investment ($ million)	Green Bank Investment ($ million)	Mobilization Ratio (Times)	Funding as Grants (%)
2022	120.1	13.3	9.0	28.0
2021	270.1	34.5	7.8	36.0
2020	286.2	33.1	8.6	45.0
2019	319.6	32.5	9.8	47.0
2018	221.8	28.5	7.8	44.0
2017	180.5	30.1	6.0	41.0
2016	320.4	38.0	8.4	52.0
2015	320.6	58.7	5.5	56.0
2014	107.1	31.8	3.4	65.0
2013	111.1	18.5	6.0	67.0
2012	9.9	3.4	2.9	100.0
Total	**2,267.4**	**322.4**	**7.0**	**49.7**

Source: Connecticut Green Bank, Annual Comprehensive Financial Report.

Noted impacts of Connecticut Green Bank include the creation of more than 26,720 direct, indirect, and induced job-years; helping generate an estimated $113.6 million in state tax revenues; accelerating the growth of renewable energy to more than 509 megawatts and 10.4 million tons of carbon dioxide or 156 million tree seedlings grown for 10 years or 2.1 million passenger vehicles driven for 1 year, improving the lives of families, helping them avoid sick days, hospital visits, and even death, and set goals to reach 40% investment in communities that may be disproportionately harmed by climate change (Connecticut Green Bank 2022).

United Kingdom Green Investment Bank

In October 2012, the UK government established the UK Green Investment Bank, the most important example of a newly established GIB. It was publicly funded and bestowed with an explicit mandate to "accelerate the UK's transition to a greener, stronger economy" by investing in green projects and mobilizing private finance into the green energy sector. Despite (or because of) its success, the Government of the UK decided to privatize it, and in March 2016, initiated a process to sell the UK GIB into private ownership. In the five years the UK GIB operated before its sale in 2017, it helped finance more than £12 billion of UK green infrastructure projects (National Audit Office 2017). Figure 7 shows how the UK GIB's investment activity increased over time. In 100 projects, it committed £3.4 billion of its capital and attracted £8.6 billion of private capital, equating to a mobilization ratio of 2.5. That is, for every £1.0 invested, it raised £2.5 of private capital. However, in 2012–13 and 2015–16, the mobilization ratio was 3.6 and 3.8, respectively—at the very start of the operation of the bank. It is reasonable to assume that the mobilization ratio could have been increased going forward, had the UK GIB not been privatized.

The GIB invested 46% of its capital in the offshore wind sector, 34% in the waste and bioenergy sector (including waste treatment and biomass gasification technologies), 14% in non-domestic energy efficiency, and 6% in onshore renewables (Figure 8). Table 6 shows the estimated green impact of the UK GIB's portfolio on 31 March 2017.

Figure 7: UK Green Investment Bank Investment Activity and Commitment of Capital

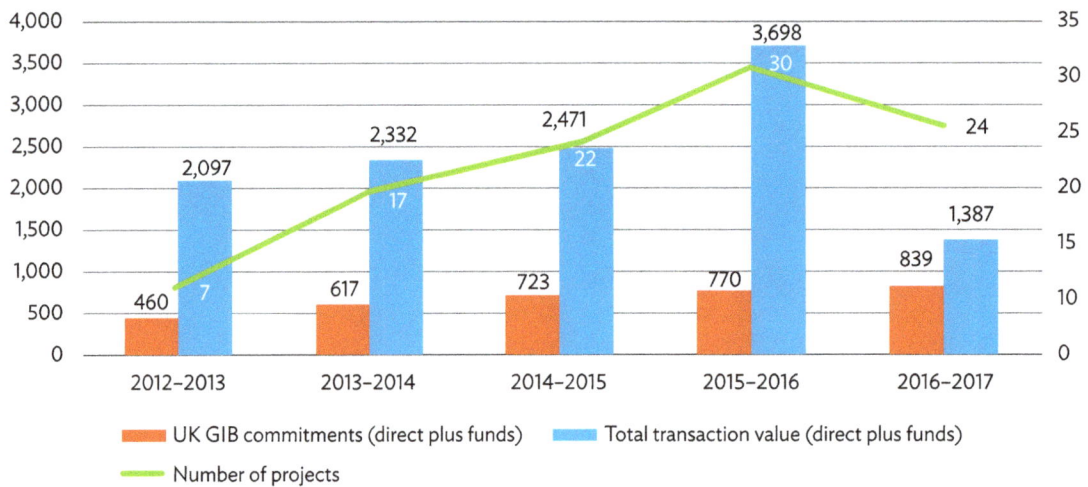

UK GIB commitments (direct plus funds)   Total transaction value (direct plus funds)
Number of projects

GIB = Green Investment Bank.

Source: Compiled with data from National Audit Office analysis of Green Investment Bank annual reports and accounts. (National Audit Office 2017).

Figure 8: The UK Green Investment Bank's Investment Portfolio at March 2017

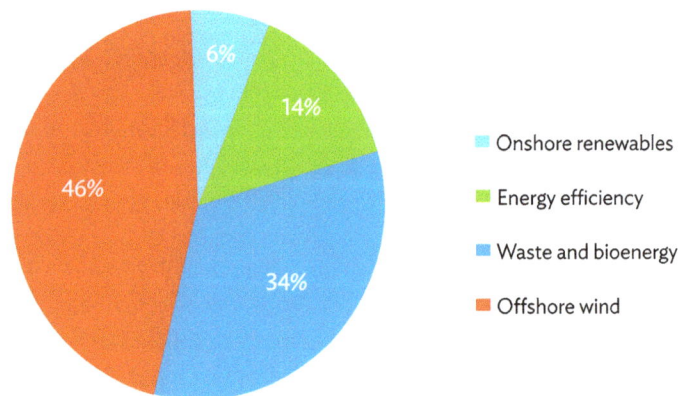

Onshore renewables

Energy efficiency

Waste and bioenergy

Offshore wind

GIB = Green Investment Bank.

Source: Compiled with data from National Audit Office analysis of Green Investment Bank annual reports and accounts. (National Audit Office 2017).

Table 6: Green Impact of UK Green Investment Bank's Portfolio on 31 March 2017

Greenhouse gas emissions reduction	t CO_2e^a '000	Percentage of the UK's annual target reduction in greenhouse gas emissions during the UK's Third Carbon Budget (2018–2022)
Green impact of GIB's portfolio in 2016–2017	7,835	16.5%
Future estimated average annual green impact	7,955	16.7%
Renewable energy generated	**GWh[b]**	**Equivalent percentage of the UK's projected renewable electricity production in 2020**
Green impact of GIB's portfolio in 2016-2017	15,606	12.8%
Future estimated average annual green impact	21,547	17.7%
Energy demand reduced[c]	**GWh[b]**	**Equivalent percentage of the UK's projected renewable electricity production in 2020**
Green impact of GIB's portfolio in 2016-2017	87	less than 0.1%
Future estimated average annual green impact	272	0.2%

[a] UK GIB reported on this figure in its annual report and accounts, it was not a core key performance indicator.

GIB = Green Investment Bank, gWh = gigawatt-hours, tCO_2e = tons of carbon dioxide equivalent, UK = United Kingdom.

Source: Compiled with data from National Audit Office analysis of Green Investment Bank annual reports and accounts (National Audit Office 2017).

In establishing the UK GIB, the government aimed to set it up as "an enduring institution" with "best practice corporate governance arrangements" and ensuring "that it operates at arm's length from Government" (HM Government 2011, 20). The UK GIB's corporate governance arrangements included:

- A well-defined charter that contains the UK GIB's mission and operating principles and provides guidance on its long-term goals.
- Clear strategic priorities that outline green priorities, sectors in scope, and high-level guidance on investment criteria.
- Investment criteria which translate the strategic priorities into metrics to guide the GIB's investment decisions.

The Government of the UK set out the following operating principles (HM Government 2011, 21):

- **Green objectives, sustainable finances**: Working toward a "double bottom line", deploying capital to achieve significant green impact while generating positive portfolio returns and, in doing so, preserving and building its capital base.
- **Enduring impact**: Building a sustainable institution that delivers the long-term impact required by the UK's transition to a green economy.

- **Strategic alignment with government**: Aligning strategic priorities with government green policy objectives and initiatives.
- **Operational independence from government**: Putting management and operational decision making at arm's length from government.
- **Partnership with the private sector**: Operating in cooperation with private sector players, enhancing private sector provision and leveraging private sector capabilities where appropriate, and not acting where government policy objectives could be met by private sector provision alone.
- **Minimizing distortions**: Operating consistently with European Union state aid rules, minimizing inappropriate competition and adverse impacts on market pricing.

Generally, the UK GIB is seen as a very successful endeavor (e.g., Matikainen 2017, Green Finance Institute 2020) which, among others, helped "successfully [de-risk] emerging offshore wind technologies, creating new financial markets, and crowding in private capital" (Green Finance Institute 2020). The UK government completed the sale of the UK GIB to the private sector investor Macquarie Group Limited in Aug 2017.[15] The important role the UK GIB played in accelerating the financing of renewables during its short time of operation is also reflected in the considerations of subsequent UK governments for establishing a new GIB (Ambrose 2020). The UK GIB's governance arrangements and operational principles can be seen as a best international practice and could be used as a template to draw from when establishing a new GIB.

Malaysia's Green Technology Financing Scheme

The Malaysian Green Technology and Climate Change Centre (formerly the Malaysian Green Technology Corporation/GreenTech Malaysia) provides loan guarantees and subsidies to encourage private banks to finance green projects through its Green Technology Financing Scheme (GTFS). It is a nonprofit government agency under the Ministry of Environment mandated to lead the nation in green growth, climate change mitigation, and climate resilience and adaptation. The special financing scheme supports the development of green technology. It assesses eligible companies' applications for "green project certificates" and provides them. A broad range of technologies and solutions are eligible for the guarantee across the energy, water and waste treatment, building, and transport sectors. Properly certified green projects or companies can seek loans from participating commercial banks, which receive a 60% loan repayment guarantee from the GTFS.

There have been three manifestations of the GTFS (Table 7). GTFS 1.0 was active from 2010 to 2017 and offered a 2% a year interest/profit rate subsidy for the first 7 years, with a 60% government guarantee of the financing. GTFS 2.0 was approved in April 2018 with a volume of up to RM5 billion, launched in May 2018, but discontinued by the new government after the general election in May 2018. In March 2019, the Malaysian Ministry of Finance decided to

---

[15] Source: News Story of the UK government: https://www.gov.uk/government/news/uk-governments-sale-of-green-investment-bank-completed. According to the announcement, the privatization is expected to bring contributions to growing its support for green projects and the transition to a green economy with overseas investment. However, there were also criticisms about the sale due to a concern such as a possibility of lack of continued green commitments.

reinstate GTFS 2.0 with the allocation of RM2 billion from January 2019 until the end of 2020. In addition to providing the GTFS 1.0 financing facilities, GTFS 2.0 provides financing through *sukuk* (green bond) issuance. GTFS 2.0 also offers financial support for energy services companies to finance investments or assets related to energy-efficient projects and/or energy performance contracting. The government launched GTFS 3.0 in 2021 as part of its agenda to support sustainable and responsible investment and to drive green and sustainable standards in Malaysia. The RM2 billion scheme now includes support for the issuance of sustainable and responsible investment *sukuk* and green bonds.

Table 7: Malaysia's Green Technology Financing Scheme

Stage	Years of operation	Volume	Operations
GTFS 1.0	2010–2017	RM4.5 billion	Loan guarantees and subsidies to private banks with 2% a year interest/profit rate subsidy for the first 7 years with a 60% government guarantee on the financing
GTFS 2.0	May 2018/2019–2020	RM5 billion/RM2 billion	GTFS 1.0 financing facilities Financing through *sukuk* (green bond) issuance Financial support for energy services companies to finance investment or assets related to energy-efficient project and/or energy performance contracting
GTFS 3.0	2021–present	RM2 billion	GTFS 1.0 and 2.0 financing facilities Support of issuance of sustainable and responsible investment *sukuk* and green bonds

GTFS = Green Technology Financing Scheme.
Source: Compiled by author.

GTFS currently has three main facilities:
- **For producers**: Up to RM100 million for up to 15 years for legally registered Malaysian companies that have at least 51% Malaysian shareholding to finance investment for the production of green products.
- **For users**: Up to RM50 million for up to 10 years for legally registered Malaysian companies that have at least 51% Malaysian shareholding to finance investment for the utilization of green technology.
- **For energy service companies**: Up to RM25 million for up to 5 years for companies legally registered in Malaysia with at least 51% Malaysian shareholding to finance investment or assets related to energy-efficient project and/or energy performance contracting.

Importantly, GTFS lending has been accompanied by other public incentives and policies, including a Green Investment Tax Allowance and a Green Income Tax Exemption scheme (MGTC 2022) to encourage green investment. While not a full-fledged GIB, GTFS has enhanced green lending and investment in Malaysia by working with commercial banks, providing a positive example of which newly created GIBs could build. However, it should be noted that there is no independent, systematic, and rigorous review of the impact of GTFS to date.[16]

---

[16] A study of five corporations in the energy sector that benefited from GTFS financing suggests that it had "a substantial impact on improving financial performance" by helping with capital expenditures and led to improvements in the companies' assets, revenues, and profits (Adebiyi et al. 2020, 1).

Japan's Green Fund and Green Innovation Fund

Japan's Green Fund commenced operations in July 2013, following the Ministry of Environment's January 2013 announcement of the Finance Initiative to Build a Low-Carbon Society, which highlighted the need to use private capital to tackle global warming. The Green Fund is governed by the Green Finance Organisation, an entity within the Japanese Ministry of the Environment. The Green Fund was capitalized by a portion of the revenue of the Tax for Climate Change Mitigation, a carbon tax established in 2012 on fossil fuel consumption. Figure 9 shows the structure of the Green Fund.

Figure 9: Structure of the Green Fund

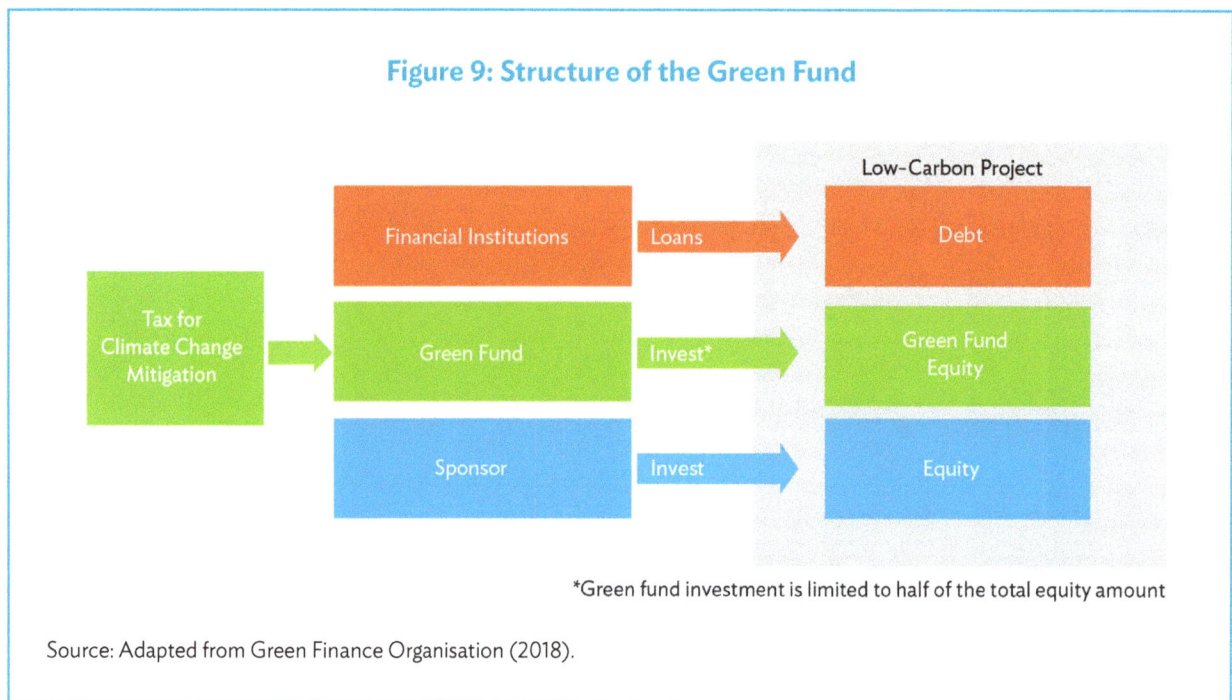

*Green fund investment is limited to half of the total equity amount

Source: Adapted from Green Finance Organisation (2018).

The Green Fund was specifically established to address the challenges associated with clean energy projects, including high up-front capital costs for development and construction as well as long operation and income phases that increase risk for project owners/developers. It seeks to solidify the business case of small- to large-scale clean energy projects by making equity and mezzanine investments that attract further capital from private sources. It supports low-carbon projects such as wind, solar, hydro, biomass, geothermal, and waste management. The Green Fund also shares information associated with projects with other project owners and private actors to aid their clear understanding of the technical and financial feasibility and sustainability of these low-carbon energy projects.

The creation of the Green Fund resulted from the need for sizable additional investments for a significant reduction of greenhouse gases, the creation of a decarbonized society, longer lead times for decarbonization projects, and the difficulty of many local businesses that are small and medium-sized enterprises to raise funds given their relatively weak capital. Its mechanism involves realizing decarbonization projects by priming private sector funds. To achieve this, the Green Fund will invest in local decarbonization projects using the tax revenue from the global warming countermeasure tax.

The purpose of the Green Fund is to create a new flow of money for the green economy and to realize a "decarbonized society" and "regional revitalization." The investment by the Green Fund will attract further investment and loans from the private sector, contributing to the realization of decarbonization projects. Realization of the decarbonization project will lead to job creation and industrial development in the region, contributing to regional revitalization.

In terms of regional revitalization, investment projects require a certain return or recovery of the investment and must meet the following requisites: (i) the project should be led by a local business operator; (ii) local employment promotion must ensue; (iii) there must be investment/financing by local stakeholders; (iv) project earnings should be returned to the local community through dividends, tax revenue, etc.; and (v) energy communities must be fostered by assuming utilization of energy by the local community, i.e., local production for local consumption.

Established by the Regional Decarbonization Investment Promotion Fund Project under the jurisdiction of the Ministry of the Environment, it was registered under the name Green Finance Promotion Organization. The main business of the organization includes conducting investigative research, collecting and provisioning information, providing consultation, and extending business support using finance for creating a low-carbon society. It also conducts businesses incidental to the main business of the organization.

Equity investments of the Green Fund are limited to less than 50% of the total equity amount, and in some cases, a sub-fund will be created that aggregates equity investments from the Green Finance Promotion Organization and other sponsors before funding the project vehicle. This investment strategy aims to decrease the debt-to-equity ratio to facilitate loan financing as well as support the deployment of new clean technologies in the green economy. Successes are publicized and used to encourage expanding green investment to regional private sectors across the country.

Investments are made in projects that not only reduce greenhouse gas emissions but also stimulate local economies. This is achieved by working with locally based companies and, in some cases, focusing particularly on the project development phase during which there is no revenue generation. The Green Finance Promotion Organization invests specifically in projects with new business models that can be replicated in regional communities. It also aims to engage with local communities, and this engagement goes beyond clean energy project deployment. Box 4 provides a summary of the select projects invested by the Japan Green Fund.

Box 4: Selected Projects of Japan's Green Fund

Kyushu Geothermal Power Generation Fund

The Green Fund committed to invest $7 million in the Kyushu Geothermal Power Generation Fund (Kyushu Renewable Energy Investment Business Limited Partnership), which is managed by Astmax Trading Inc. The Fund invests in geothermal power, hot springs power, and solar power renewable energy businesses in Kyushu. It was established with an initial commitment of $14.1 million, comprising an investment of $7 million by the Green Fund, and $7.01 million by Astmax Trading, Inc. and Astmax Co., Ltd. The Fund is managed by Astmax Trading Inc as a general partner with unlimited liability.

Community Solar, Niigata

The Green Fund committed to invest $0.7 million in a solar power photovoltaic generation project planned by Oratte Niigata Community Energy Council. This was the first Regional Support Investment made by the Green Fund. The Council was launched in December 2014 to promote the take-up of renewable energy with a focus on the local community, following a study group set up by Niigata City into regional area power generation with the participation of local residents. This project is a small-scale distributed solar photovoltaic power generation business, which uses ground sites, the rooftops of local public buildings and private companies, as well as factory rooftops and vacant land in Niigata.

Small Hydro, Okayama

The Green Fund committed to invest $0.8 million of equity in a small hydro project in Okayama. In this project, Nishi Awakura village of the local government became the main sponsor and established a special corporation for the project. The project develops a new private-sector small hydropower plant, utilizing the abundant water resources of the Yoshino River crossing the village. Nishi Awakura village in the business site is located at the northernmost tip of Okayama, and has a population of about 1,500 with a population decline and an aging population. This local government project showcases a regional model that maximizes the use of regional resources and achieves both low-carbon sustainability and sustainable development. This project, along with existing village hydropower plants, helps to achieve the goal of Nishikakura village to generate 40% of its electricity needs through hydroelectric.

Source: Adapted from the Green Bank Network.

Following the declaration of the goal to reach carbon neutrality in the Japanese economy by 2050, in October 2020, the Ministry of Economy, Trade and Industry decided to launch a Green Innovation Fund with ¥2 trillion as part of the New Energy and Industrial Technology Development Organization. The 2050 CN Declaration is significantly more ambitious than previous Japanese governmental policies for carbon neutrality, and to achieve this goal, the structural transformation of the energy and industrial sectors and innovation through bold investments will need to be greatly accelerated.

The Green Innovation Fund seeks to fund research and development activities that can deliver technological advances that will help the net-zero transition. To this end, the ministry formulated "basic policies" for the Green Innovation Fund (Figure 10). The Ministry of Economy, Trade and Industry inaugurated the Committee on the Green Innovation Project in February 2021. The fund was set up to provide 10 years of continuous support to business-led decarbonization initiatives, ranging from research and development and demonstration to social implementation, with ambitious and specific goals shared between the public and private sectors.

Figure 10: Basic Policies of the Green Innovation Fund

1 Purpose and Outline

To achieve carbon neutrality by 2050, **METI established a ¥2 trillion fund as part of NEDO** and provide **continuous support for R&D projects, demonstrations, and social implementation projects for 10 years to companies that commit to ambitious goals.**

2 Program Target

(Per project)
Ambitious 2030 Target
(Performance, Cost etc.)

MonitorCross-sectoral monitoring of fund projects based on the following;
*International Competitiveness
*Commercialization (TRL, etc.)
*Potential for attracting private investment

• CO_2 Reduction Effect
• Economic Effect

3 Support Target

METI's support will focus on **priority fields for which implementation plans have been formulated within the Green Growth Strategy, where policy effects are significant, and long-term continous support is required to realize public implementation.**

✓ Average size of conventional R&D projects (¥20 billion) or more.
✓ Projects for which short-term government support programs is sufficient are not eligible.
✓ Main implementers should be companies or other profit-making businesses capable of carrying out the entire process of public implementation (participation of small and medium-sized venture companies is encouraged; participation of universities and research institutions is also expected).
✓ The project must include innovative and fundamental R&D elements that are worthy of being commissioned by the government.

4 Strategy for Maximizing Results

To ensure that research and development results are steadily implemented publicly, METI seek **the commitment of the managers of companies and other organizations to persevere in challenging these goals as long-term business issues.**

(Efforts required of company managers)
*Submission of the vision and the long-term business strategy at the time of application
*Attendance and report to the WG
*Submission of a management sheet showing the status of initiatives

(Implementation of a system to enhance commitment)
1) If the status of the project is inadequate, the project will be canceled, and a portion of the consignment fee will be returned.
2) Introduction of a system (an incentive measure) that allows the government to pay more depending on the degree of achievement of targets.

5 Scheme — Build a highly transparent and effective governance system that incorporates the knowledge of external experts and close cooperation among related organizations.

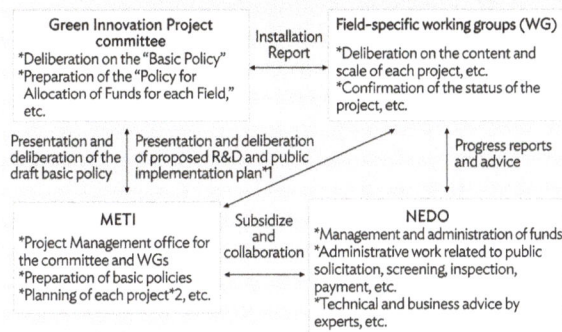

4 Program Schedule

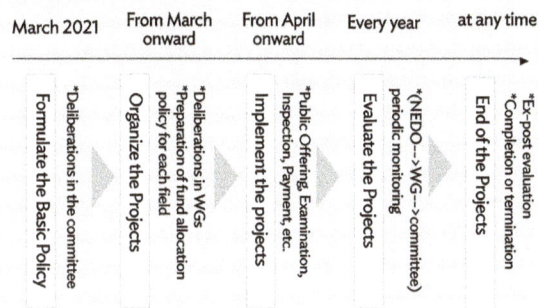

1 A plan describing the project's goals for 2030, R&D items, maturity level of the target technologies (TRL, etc.), budget scale, etc. (A draft of the plan is discussed by the WG.)
2 Including the division office in charge of the project in the relevant ministry or agency.

Notes: CO_2 = carbon dioxide; METI = Ministry of Economy, Trade and Industry; NEDO = New Energy and Industrial Technology Development Organization; R&D = Research and Development; WG = Working Groups.

Source: Japan'xs METI (Ministry of Economy, Trade and Industry).

The Green Innovation Fund will support the following priority areas for which action plans have been formulated in the Green Development Strategy, focusing on areas where the effects of governmental policies may be significant and where long-term, continuous support will be needed with a view to social implementation:

- Energy-related industries—offshore wind, solar and geothermal, hydrogen, fuel and ammonia, next-generation thermal energy and nuclear;

- Transportation and manufacturing-related industries—automotive and battery storage, semiconductor and telecommunications, shipbuilding, logistics, circulation of individuals and civil infrastructure, food, agriculture, forestry and fisheries, aircraft, carbon recycling and materials; and
- Home and office-related industries—housing and building, next generation power management, resource recycling and lifestyle.

In addition, one of the features of the Green Innovation Fund is that, in order to maximize the results, the following measures are taken to ensure a strong commitment from the management of the companies receiving support from the Fund to tackle decarbonizing challenges:

- Cancellation of the project and partial return of commissioned funds in the event of inadequate efforts.
- Introduction of incentives such as a contingency fee, in which the percentage of the costs borne by the government varies depending on the degree of achievement of the targets set for the management and other factors.

Advocating for the promotion of hydrogen use over the next 10 years, the Green Innovation Fund's first project, a hydrogen-related project developing technologies for transportation, storage and power generation with a view to establishing an international hydrogen supply chain, started in August 2021. Several projects have already been selected to receive support from the fund, including the following seven projects related to hydrogen and ammonia:

- Establishment of a fuel ammonia supply chain
- Utilization of hydrogen in the steelmaking process
- Development of next-generation ships (hydrogen-fueled ships, ammonia-fueled ships, etc.)
- Development of next-generation aircrafts (hydrogen aircrafts)
- Development of plastic raw material production technologies using, among others, hydrogen and CO_2
- Hydrogen production by water electrolysis using electricity derived from renewable energy among other sources
- Development of technologies for transportation, storage and power generation for the establishment of an international hydrogen supply chain

As Japan has been a world leader in the development of hydrogen-related technologies and the introduction of hydrogen-related policies, the Green Innovation Fund is considered an important policy tool for strengthening Japan's international competitiveness in a decarbonized society, following the international momentum toward this move.

VII. Developing Green Investment Banks in Asia and the Pacific

As discussed in Section 2, the climate investment and SDG financing gap in Asia and the Pacific is enormous. Public development banks, of which there is no shortage, and GIBs will have to play a key role in closing this gap. According to the Global Database on Public Development Banks and Development Financing Institutions, 139 public development banks operate nationally or sub-nationally in Asia and the Pacific with total assets exceeding $6.9 trillion in 2020 (Xu et al. 2021, updated version: November 2022). For the time being, however, very few of these have a green footprint. While awareness has been rising of the need to account for environmental, social, and governance factors, public development bank portfolios—just like those of commercial banks—are far from aligned with climate and environmental goals.

The need is urgent to phase out financing of environmentally harmful projects—most notably coal and other fossil fuel projects—and instead scale up the financing of green projects. This is true for all financial institutions—commercial or public development banks—but the latter, as publicly mandated institutions, should indeed take the lead. Furthermore, a strong case exists for developing specialized GIBs across Asia with the expertise to develop and finance green projects at scale. Regionally, as mentioned, ADB aspires to be "Asia and the Pacific's Climate Bank." Nationally, governments should look at either transforming existing national development banks into dedicated GIBs or consider establishing new GIBs from scratch.

As Section 4 discusses, there are trade-offs between the greening of an existing national development bank and the creation of a new GIB. Careful analysis is required—not least of political economy factors—whether attempts at transforming an existing institution into a GIB are likely to succeed. Rigorous assessment is needed: not all national development banks are operating successfully, and not all can be transformed into successful GIBs. Trying to reform an ailing institution with legacy problems may well turn out to be a waste of time and resources. Conversely, a well-managed national development bank (ideally with an existing portfolio of green projects) where both the staff and the leadership are committed to such a transformation could become a superior alternative than creating a new institution, which will inevitably take time to get operational.

International development finance institutions should consider establishing two support mechanisms:

- **A support program for existing national development banks to transform into GIB**: This would involve analysis of the potential for turning existing national development banks into GIBs, the feasibility of such a transition, and the capital and staffing needs to make this happen. A strategy would be needed, including options for capitalization and debt financing, and a plan developed for hiring new expert staff and training existing staff. If a decision is taken to move ahead with a transition, development finance institutions could help the national development bank in implementing its transition strategy.

- **A support program for establishing new GIB**s: International development finance institutions could provide strategic advice to their developing country member governments on the establishment of new GIBs and the best strategy to make this happen. This would have to involve a feasibility study and an operational strategy including a financial plan and a human resources strategy. As discussed, development finance institutions could play a key role in capitalizing the GIB or otherwise provide credit enhancement to help it achieve a lower cost of capital.

Lessons could be learned from the establishment of the UK GIB for both the transition of an existing national development bank into a GIB as well as the creation of a new GIB from scratch. In particular, the UK GIB provides a template for the following:

- A well-defined charter with a clear mission and operating principles that can guide the GIB's long-term goals.
- The setting of clear strategic priorities that outline priority sectors and high-level guidance on investment criteria.
- The development of investment criteria which translate the strategic priorities into metrics to guide the GIB's investment decisions.

Moreover, development finance institutions could help national development banks and/or GIBs build expertise among staff in green financing and project development through capacity building programs and staff exchanges, inviting staff from the national development banks and/or GIBs for secondments and sending their own staff for such secondments as well.

VIII. Issues, Challenges, and Considerations

Given the enormous investment needs in adaptation and the green and just transformation, there is a large need for GIBs with a clear mandate and strong capacities to accelerate climate action. GIBs can be established by either transforming existing national development banks into GIBs by updating their mandates (and possibly linking this with a capital increase) or by creating entirely new GIBs. MDBs and development finance institutions can support the establishment of new GIBs and help existing national development banks reinvent themselves as GIBs and play a larger role in climate and SDG finance. They can do this in two ways: (i) by offering technical assistance to help build strong governance structures and expertise in financing green infrastructure and projects and (ii) by helping GIBs strengthen their standing in capital markets by providing capital, guarantees, or credit enhancement that will enable GIBs to obtain higher ratings and lower refinancing costs.

By doing so, MDBs and international development finance institutions can harness the potential of GIBs to overcome investment barriers, leverage private capital, and play an important role in financing infrastructure development and advancing a just transition to a low-carbon, climate-resilient economy. At the same time, GIBs can act as important local partners for MDBs and international development finance institutions by building local expertise and supporting national governments in developing pro-climate policy and investment frameworks. For a multilateral institution like ADB, GIBs can play a key role in helping to intensify its cooperation with developing member countries to achieve its climate ambition and provide $100 billion of climate finance to developing Asia by 2030 (Box 5).

Box 5: Examples of ADB Operations in Supporting Climate and Sustainable Development Goal Finance

Loans

Indonesia. In Southeast Asia, ADB is supporting the Sustainable Development Goals Indonesia One–Green Finance Facility (SIO-GFF) to help the country meet the Sustainable Development Goals (SDGs) and achieve a green recovery.[a] The $150 million loan to the government will be relent to PT Sarana Multi Infrastruktur (Persero) (PT SMI), a state-owned infrastructure financing institution. The facility will finance subprojects that meet green, financial bankability, and leverage targets with the aim of catalyzing funds from private institutions and commercial sources. Funds will be provided primarily as debt to subprojects, but up to 15% of total committed funds may be provided as other instruments such as equity, convertible debt, and guarantees. It is the first green finance facility in Southeast Asia.

continued on next page

Box 5 *continued*

The facility applies three key design principles:

- Clear green or SDG eligibility criteria and measurable indicators for subproject selection
- Clear subproject bankability targets (minimum debt service coverage ratio of 1.05 and a positive net present value) to be achieved with SIO-GFF support
- Catalytic requirement for at least 30% of private, institutional and commercial capital to be mobilized for each green subproject (20% for non-green SDG subprojects)

In addition to the loan, technical assistance is provided to enhance PT SMI's subproject pipelines and monitoring systems; strengthen green and SDG subproject pipelines and government capacity; and develop future phase and road maps for SIO-GFF.

ADB loan funds will partially finance up to 10 projects worth $423 million[b] catalyzing around 3 times private capital into the subprojects. Moreover, if funds are recycled for two investment cycles, an investment volume of approximately $1 billion could be generated, providing a leverage of about 8 times the ADB loan amount. Loan funds are also estimated to provide at least $137 million for both climate mitigation and adaptation and reduce CO_2 emissions by 480,700 tons per annum.

The infographic summary below provides key and innovative features about the project.

Technical Assistance

ASEAN+3. ADB serves as the secretariat for the Asian Bond Markets Initiative (ABMI), which was launched by the Association of Southeast Asian Nations (ASEAN) plus the People's Republic of China (PRC), Japan, and the Republic of Korea (ASEAN+3) in December 2002. ABMI aims to (i) foster the development of local currency bond markets as an alternative source of funding to short-term foreign currency loans, and (ii) promote regional financial cooperation and integration for a more resilient financial system.

As part of this initiative, ADB has been providing technical assistance to promote green local currency-denominated bonds for infrastructure development. Approved in March 2020, the Creating Ecosystems for Green Local Currency Bonds for Infrastructure Development in ASEAN+3 builds on the recommendations of an earlier study to support the successful issuance of green local currency bonds.[c] The project helps issuers identify eligible assets, develop a sustainable bond framework, and engage external reviewers. To develop the ecosystem, local service providers are also capacitated to become local green bond verifiers. As a result, three local credit rating agencies have been accredited by the Climate Bonds Initiative.

As of November 2022, the TA has helped to mobilize more than $800 million of ESG financing, including the first social bond issued by a nonfinancial corporate issuer in Thailand (B1 billion or $30.5 million) and the first green bond in Cambodia (KR6 billion or $1.5 million).

continued on next page

Box 5 *continued*

Key and Innovative Features of Sustainable Development Goals Indonesia One–Green Finance Facility

SDG Indonesia One: Green Finance Facility
$150 million ADB Financial Intermediation Loan

Innovative and Integrated Design for Accelerating Green Recovery in Indonesia

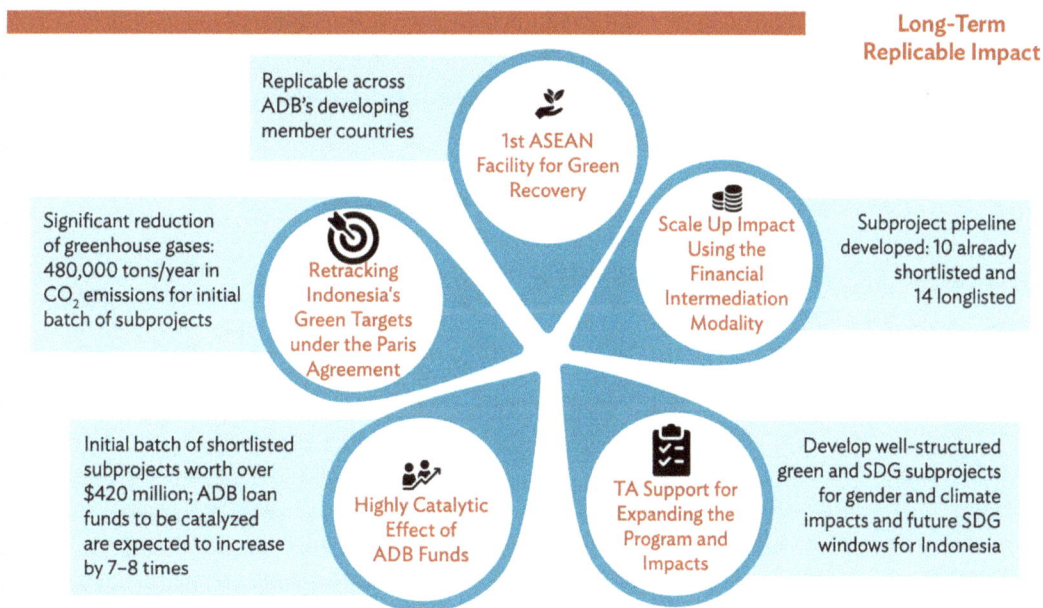

Pipeline Acceleration
TA funds for deepening green and SDG project preparation and pipeline – 10 subprojects

De-risking Funds Approach
Loan funds for improving green and SDG subproject bankability

Equity Participation
Deepening commercial fund flows

Globally Aligned Green and SDG Frameworks
For subproject selection and impact

Leveraging Conditionalities
To mobilize private capital into subprojects

Strategic Partnership with PT SMI
Green and blue finance, PPP and provincial sector

Long-Term Replicable Impact

Replicable across ADB's developing member countries

1st ASEAN Facility for Green Recovery

Significant reduction of greenhouse gases: 480,000 tons/year in CO_2 emissions for initial batch of subprojects

Retracking Indonesia's Green Targets under the Paris Agreement

Scale Up Impact Using the Financial Intermediation Modality

Subproject pipeline developed: 10 already shortlisted and 14 longlisted

Initial batch of shortlisted subprojects worth over $420 million; ADB loan funds to be catalyzed are expected to increase by 7–8 times

Highly Catalytic Effect of ADB Funds

TA Support for Expanding the Program and Impacts

Develop well-structured green and SDG subprojects for gender and climate impacts and future SDG windows for Indonesia

ADB = Asian Development Bank, ASEAN = Association of Southeast Asian Nations, CO_2 = carbon dioxide, DMC = developing member country, FI = financial intermediation, GHG = greenhouse gas, PPP = public–private partnership, PT SMI = PT Sarana Multi Infrastruktur (Persero), SDG = Sustainable Development Goal, TA = technical assistance.
Source: Asian Development Bank.

continued on next page

Box 5 *continued*

South Asia. A knowledge and support technical assistance for South Asia was approved in June 2019. The Deploying Solar Systems at Scale project is being implemented as part of ADB's cooperation arrangement with the International Solar Alliance. A treaty-based international organization, the alliance aims to mobilize more than $1 trillion into solar power by 2030. The project will identify and develop a pipeline of solar energy projects, including improving their bankability so that public sector funds leverage commercial investment. In addition, it will also identify and scale up financing instruments for solar deployment. In February 2023, the alliance and Bangladesh Ministry of Power Energy and Mineral Resources signed a joint country partnership strategy and plans.

[a] Average of 35% per subproject.
[b] ADB. Indonesia: Sustainable Development Goals Indonesia One – Green Finance Facility (Phase 1) (4172-INO). Manila.

There are also challenges in establishing GIBs, as they restrict their business transactions with entities that qualify in their rigorous screening processes, limiting their support base. Also, building new institutions or transforming existing ones into GIBs will take time. It will hence take several years for them to maximize their potential. Higher operating costs are expected since they are tapping talented and experienced staff with local and national expertise in dealing with green businesses and customers.

Newly established GIBs can help scale up green investment in Asia and the Pacific developing countries. GIBs can be powerful and cost-effective vehicles to overcome investment barriers and leverage the impact of available public and private resources. They can catalyze private operations and capital, scale up climate financing, and localize the SDGs and green operations. GIBs can leverage public funds while maximizing total investment by partnering with private resources. Importantly, they can showcase the viability of innovative green investments. GIBs can help transform the financial sector by mainstreaming environmental, social, and governance principles and establishing best practices. They can act as local partners and investors in low-carbon, climate-resilient projects, driving project developers and investors to adopt impact metrics in tracking progress toward national climate and sustainability targets. GIBs are in the best position to assist policymakers in creating better enabling environments for low-carbon, climate-resilient projects and the formulation and achievement of their nationally determined contributions.

In summary, this paper highlights the emerging importance of GIBs to finance a transition to a just, green, and more resilient economy. It has discussed ways of strengthening the role of GIBs and how their potential can be unleashed to scale up green investments and address challenges to project-based mobilization of private capital. With the enormous need for financing to support climate-adjusted infrastructure investment in transportation, power, water, sanitation, and telecommunications, investments made by GIBs can leverage domestic and international private capital to finance climate-related actions that support the SDGs. This means, however, that MDBs and national development banks must create an enabling environment and a strong framework to catalyze green investments and streamline their investment projects that target green finance while overcoming market failures.

GIBs, as discussed in this paper, are critical in transforming markets by stimulating low-carbon investments and accelerating market development where they can attract private investment and improve the risk-return profile. The paper highlighted the essential role of GIBs in scaling up sustainable finance aligned with the SDGs, improving financing mechanisms, harnessing better use of data and taxonomies for better impact measurement, and promoting effective collaboration and external support. The case studies presented showcased the important contributions that GIBs can make and underscored the potential of GIBs that can be released through the support of international development finance institutions. To advance just transitions in the Global South, the paper called on international development finance institutions to assist in the establishment of new GIBs or support governments converting existing institutions into GIBs.

Moving forward, a key consideration is whether to build a new GIB from scratch or work with an existing institution. "Greening" an existing national development bank may be preferable to creating a new institution when the established institution is well-governed and when the necessary institutional and political support exists. For example, many countries have national development banks (public investment, infrastructure, or industrial development banks) which focus on domestic investment. While many national development banks are less focused on mobilizing green investment than GIBs, some national development banks have been providing financing for low-carbon projects for many years, operations they can build on and extend. For example, Germany's KfW has been investing in environmental protection domestically and internationally since the 1980s, moving closer to becoming a GIB. Yet in cases where there is no incumbent institution that could be transformed into a GIB, or where existing institutions suffer from serious governance flaws, trying to transform those may be a waste of time and resources.

In either case, it is important to ensure that the GIB operates at arms-length from the government to prevent undue political interference in financing decisions. Maintaining an independent status can provide flexibility to experiment, innovate, and adapt to market developments. Immunizing GIBs also requires that they are supervised by the central bank or regulatory authority, along with strengthened systems of governance that incorporate best practice principles such as independent boards of directors and binding codes of corporate governance to ensure transparency and best practice risk management systems. In this regard, multilateral development banks and bilateral development finance institutions can play critical roles in promoting such good practices as a prerequisite for providing capital or additional funding lines that will enable GIBs to pursue their mandated goal of financing just transitions.

Appendix: Examples of Public Development Banks (International and by Economy)

Level	Name of Bank
Multinational (Global)	World Bank Group (International Bank for Reconstruction and Development, International Development Agency, International Finance Corporation, Multilateral Investment Guarantee Agency), New Development Bank
Multinational (Regional)	European Investment Bank, Asian Development Bank, Inter-American Development Bank, European Bank for Reconstruction and Development, African Development Bank, Development Bank of Latin America, Nordic Investment Bank, Islamic Development Bank, Asian Infrastructure Investment Bank, African Export and Import Bank, Central American Bank for Economic Integration, Africa Finance Corporation, West African Development Bank, Eurasian Development Bank, Arab Bank for Economic Development in Africa, Caribbean Development Bank, Development Bank of Central African States, East African Development Bank, Pacific Island Development Bank
National	Small Medium Enterprise Development Bank Malaysia Berhad, Export-Import Bank of Malaysia Berhad, Development Bank of Mongolia, Bangladesh Development Bank, Bangladesh House Building Finance Corporation, Fiji Development Bank, National Development Bank of Papua New Guinea, Nepal Infrastructure Bank, Federated States of Micronesia Development Bank, Development Bank of Samoa, Bank of the Cook Islands, Marshall Islands Development Banks, National Development Bank of Palau, Development Bank of Tuvalu, Vanuatu Agricultural Development Bank, Development Bank of Kiribati, Development Bank of Solomon Islands
Sub-economy	Promotional Bank of North Rhine-Westphalia, Economic and Infrastructure Bank Hessen, Investment Bank Berlin, Hong Kong Mortgage Corporation, Development Bank of Saxony, Bank of North Dakota, Thuringian Construction bank, Socredo Bank, Sabah Development Bank, Development Bank of Minas Gerais S.A., Rhode Island Infrastructure Bank, Development Bank of Wales, Municipality Credit Iceland, California Infrastructure and Economic Development Bank, Kerala Financial Corporation, Karnataka State Financial Corporation, Rajasthan Finance Corporation, Punjab Financial Corporation, Development Bank of American Samoa

Source: Author using the Global Database on Public Development Banks and Development Financing Institutions (Xu et al. 2021, updated version: November 2022).

References

Adebiyi, O.O., N. Mohamad, M.H. Isa, N. Samsudin, and M.T. Dela Cruz. 2020. Impact of Malaysian Green Technology Financial Scheme on Business Performance of Renewable Energy Producers. *Journal of Southwest Jiaotong University*. 55 (6).

Asian Development Bank (ADB). 2017. *Meeting Asia's Infrastructure Needs*. Manila.

Agence Française de Développement (AFD). 2023. Public Development Banks Explained in Four Infographics. Paris: AFD.

Almeida, H., I. Cunha, M.A. Ferreira, and F. Restrepo. 2017. The Real Effects of Credit Ratings: The Sovereign Ceiling Channel. *Journal of Finance*. 72 (1). pp. 249–290.

Ambrose, J. 2020. UK Government Planning New Green Investment Bank. *The Guardian*. 15 July.

Attridge, S. and L. Engen. 2019. *Blended Finance in the Poorest Countries. The Need for a Better Approach*. London: Overseas Development Institute.

Beirne, J., N. Renzhi, and U. Volz. 2021. Local Currency Bond Markets, Foreign Investor Participation, and Capital Flow Volatility in Emerging Asia. *Singapore Economic Review*. 66 (3).

Buhr, B., U. Volz, C. Donovan, G. Kling, Y. Lo, V. Murinde, and N. Pullin. 2018. Climate Change and the Cost of Capital in Developing Countries. London and Geneva: Imperial College London, SOAS University of London, UN Environment.

Carney, M. 2015. *Breaking the Tragedy of the Horizon – Climate Change and Financial Stability*. Speech by Mark Carney, Governor of the Bank of England and Chairman of the Financial Stability Board, at Lloyd's of London, London, 29 September.

Carstens, A. and H. Shin. 2019. Emerging Markets Aren't Out of the Woods Yet. *Foreign Affairs*. 15 March.

Chakrabarti, S., M. Bains, and A. Prizzon. 2022. Future Directions for the World Bank and the Broader MDB System: Some Reflections. *ODI Insights*. London: Overseas Development Institute.

Coalition for Green Capital. n.d. *What is a Green Bank*.

Connecticut Green Bank. 2022. *Solutions for Connecticut. A Model for the Nation.* 2022 Annual Report. Hartford, CT: Connecticut Green Bank.

European Investment Bank (EIB). 2020. *EIB Group Climate Bank Roadmap 2021–2025.* Luxembourg.

Finance in Common and United Nations Development Programme (UNDP). 2022. *Joint Report: The Role of Public Development Banks in Scaling Sustainable Financing.* New York: United Nations Development Programme.

Green Climate Fund (GCF). 2022. *Approved Project Preparation Facility Application: Blue-Green Investment Corporation.* Incheon: Green Climate Fund.

Green Finance Institute. 2020. *The UK Needs a Second Green Investment Bank to Help Investors Decarbonise.*

Green Finance Organisation 2018. *Accelerating Green Investment in Japan. Innovative Financing for Sustainability.* Tokyo: Green Finance Organisation.

Griffith-Jones, S. 2020. National Development Finance in Middle-Income Countries: The Role of National Development Banks. In J.A. Alonso and J.A. Ocampo, eds. *Trapped in the Middle? Developmental Challenges for Middle-Income Countries.* Oxford: Oxford University Press. pp. 233–251.

Griffith-Jones, S. 2022. The Key Roles of Development Banks in Financing the Structural Transformation. In D. Schoenmaker and U. Volz, eds. *Scaling Up Sustainable Finance and Investment in the Global South.* London: CEPR Press. pp. 105–108.

Griffith-Jones, S., S. Attridge, and M. Gouett. 2020. *Securing Climate Finance Through National Development Banks.* London: Overseas Development Institute.

HM Government. 2011. *Update on the Design of the Green Investment Bank.* London: UK Government, Department for Business, Innovation and Skills.

Humphrey, C. and A. Prizzon. 2020. *Scaling Up Multilateral Bank Finance for the COVID-19 Recovery.* ODI Insights. London: Overseas Development Institute.

International Energy Agency (IEA). 2022. *World Energy Outlook 2022.* Paris.

Kenny, C. 2022. *Billions to Trillions is (Still) Dead. What Next?* Center for Global Development Blog. 28 April.

Kling, G., Y.C. Lo, V. Murinde, and U. Volz. 2018. Climate Vulnerability and the Cost of Debt. *SOAS Centre for Global Finance Working Paper.* No.12/2018. SOAS. University of London: London.

Kraemer, M., U. Volz, and D. Schoenmaker. 2022. *Build Now, Pay Later: Frontloading Poor Countries' Climate Mitigation Investment*. VoxEU Column. 11 October.

Marodon, R. 2021. Can Development Banks Step Up to the Challenge of Sustainable Development? *Review of Political Economy*. 34 (2). pp. 268–285.

Marois, T. 2021. *Public Banks: Decarbonisation, Definancialisation and Democratisation*. Cambridge: Cambridge University Press.

Mason, J.W. 2016. *Understanding Short-Termism. Questions and Consequences*. New York: Roosevelt Institute.

Matikainen, S. 2017. *GIB Going, Going, Gone! The Future of the Green Investment Bank and Sustainable Investment in the UK*. LSE Grantham Institute Commentary. 18 August.

Malaysian Green Technology and Climate Change Corporation (MGTC). 2022. *Green Technology Tax Incentive Guidelines*. Jakarta.

Ministry of Economy Trade and Industry (METI). 2021. *The Basic Policies for the Project for the Green Innovation Fund*. Tokyo: Ministry of Economy, Trade and Industry. 12 March.

National Audit Office. 2017. *The Green Investment Bank*. Report by the Comptroller and Auditor General. London: Department for Business, Energy & Industrial Strategy, UK Government Investments.

Nelson, R.M. 2020. *Multilateral Development Banks: Overview and Issues for Congress*. Washington, DC: Congressional Research Service.

Organisation for Economic Co-operation and Development (OECD). 2015. *Green Investment Banks*. Policy Perspectives. Paris.

OECD. 2016. *Green Investment Banks: Scaling up Private Investment in Low-Carbon, Climate-Resilient Infrastructure, Green Finance and Investment*. Paris.

OECD. 2017. Green Investment Banks. Innovative Public Financial Institutions Scaling up Private, Low-Carbon Investment. *OECD Environment Policy Paper*, No. 6. Paris.

S&P Global. 2015. General Criteria: Rating Government-Related Entities: Methodology and Assumptions. RatingsDirect, 25 March.

Schub, J. 2019. *Why We Need Finance to Fight Climate Change*. Yale Insights. 27 August.

Sims, D., S. Dougherty, B. Bergöö, L. Kerr, and S. Swann. 2017. *National Development Banks and Green Investment Banks: Mobilizing Finance in Latin America and the Caribbean Toward the Implementation of Nationally Determined Contributions*. New York: Natural Resources Defense Council.

Smallridge, D., B. Buchner, C. Trabacchi, M. Netto, J.J.G. Lorenzo, and L. Serra. 2013. *The Role of National Development Banks in Catalyzing International Climate Finance*. Washington, DC: Inter-American Development Bank.

Stiglitz, J.E. 1994. The Role of the State in Financial Markets. Proceedings of the World Bank Annual Conference on Development Economics 1993. *The World Bank Economic Review*. 7 (S1). pp. 19–52.

Stiglitz, J.E. and A. Weiss. 1981. Credit Rationing in Markets with Imperfect Information. *The American Economic Review*. 71 (3). pp. 393–410.

United Nations Economic and Social Commission for Asia and the Pacific (UN ESCAP). 2019. *Economic and Social Survey of Asia and the Pacific 2019: Ambitions Beyond Growth*. Bangkok: UNESCAP.

Volz, U. and P. Knaack. 2023. Inclusive Green Finance: A New Agenda for Central Banks and Financial Supervisors. *INSPIRE Sustainable Central Banking Briefing Paper* No. 12. London: LSE Grantham Institute and SOAS Centre for Sustainable Finance.

Volz, U., P. Knaack, J. Nyman, L. Ramos, and J. Moling. 2020. *Inclusive Green Finance: From Concept to Practice*. Kuala Lumpur and London: Alliance for Financial Inclusion and SOAS. University of London.

Volz, U. and D. Schoenmaker. 2022. Scaling Up Sustainable Finance and Investment in the Global South. In D. Schoenmaker and U. Volz, eds. *Scaling Up Sustainable Finance and Investment in the Global South*. London: CEPR Press. pp. 1–8.

Xu, J., R. Marodon, X. Ru, X. Ren, and X. Wu. 2021. What are Public Development Banks and Development Financing Institutions? Qualification Criteria, Stylized Facts and Development Trends. *China Economic Quarterly International*. 1 (4). pp. 271–294 (updated version: November 2022).